658
.3123
FIE
KC Your work from home life : redefine, reo
27.95

W9-BXN-820

YOUR WORK from HOME LIFE

YOUR WORK from HOME LIFE

Redefine, Reorganize and Reinvent Your Remote Work

M.J. FIEVRE AND BECCA ANDERSON

Coral Gables

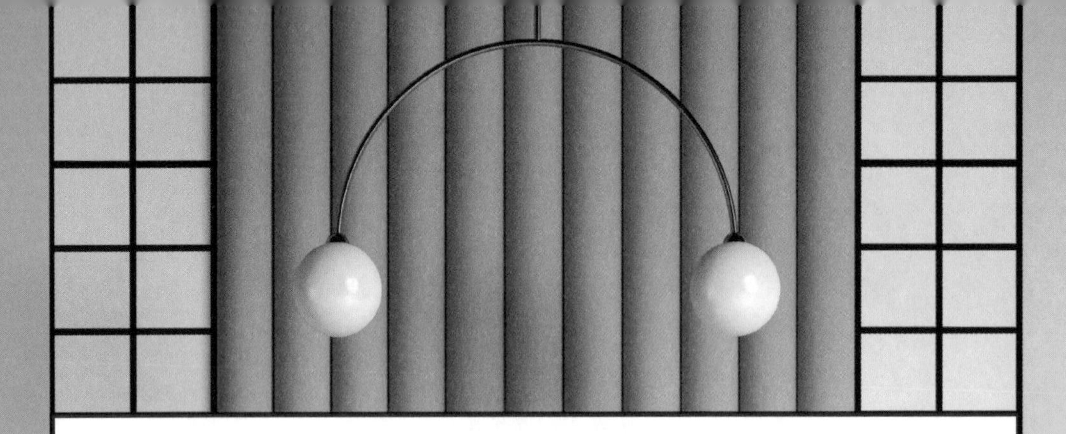

Cover Design: Roberto Nuñez

Interior Layout Design: Jermaine Lau

Published by Conari Press, an imprint of Mango Publishing, a division of Mango Media Inc.

For permission requests, please contact the publisher at:

Mango Publishing Group
2850 Douglas Road, 2nd Floor
Coral Gables, FL 33134 USA
info@mango.bz

For special orders, quantity sales, course adoptions and corporate sales, please email the publisher at sales@mango.bz. For trade and wholesale sales, please contact Ingram Publisher Services at customer.service@ingramcontent.com or +1.800.509.4887.

Your Work from Home Life: Redefine, Reorganize and Reinvent Your Remote Work

ISBN: (p) 978-1-64250-490-3 (e) 978-1-64250-491-0

BISAC: BUS097000, BUSINESS & ECONOMICS / Workplace Culture

LCCN: 2020951518

Printed in the United States of America.

TABLE OF CONTENTS

A
Monday

INTRODUCTION

Technological advances have made it possible for more workers than ever to give up their long, frustrating commutes to nine-to-five jobs. Instead of languishing in crowded offices, employees can work from the comfort of their own homes. Not only are more employers offering their workers remote positions, more people are creating their own opportunities for nontraditional work. If you are reading this book, chances are you are one of the many people who have either shifted to a remote career or are considering it. Welcome to the world of telecommuting!

Whether you are already a remote employee, a freelancer, a consultant who is looking to boost productivity and troubleshoot distractions, or someone who dreams of giving up the daily grind for a career of their own design, *Your Work From Home Life* is the book you need to reorganize and redefine your career.

Whatever your aspirations for a work-at-home career, it is our hope that you'll find this book fun and uplifting and that you'll put to good use the checklists and templates we provide. They're meant to help you maintain your health and sanity by adding joy to your workday and help you take advantage of technology and platforms. In these pages, you'll find tips and templates for home office setups, time and distraction management, discipline, and (a lot of) self-care. In addition to planning, budgeting, and so on, *Your Work From Home Life* focuses on ways to love yourself because working from home requires that you practice self-improvement and become centered.

This book will help you understand the pros and cons of working from home, learn to maintain strong bonds with your colleagues while redefining collegial camaraderie, clearly establish boundaries between home and work, avoid becoming overwhelmed and isolated, and learn how to handle an emergency or crisis. It will also allow you to help your managers by prioritizing and staying focused and on task in order to meet pressing deadlines and to research your competition, discover new ideas and skills, and provide value to your ideal customer.

The authors of this book have wisdom to spare in the work from home field. **M.J.** has many years of experience working in nontraditional and remote roles as an educator, writer, coach, translator, and entrepreneur. She currently works as an acquisitions editor for the fastest-growing publisher in the United States and serves as a project manager for a multifaceted corporation with a multinational consultant base that provides art, writing, and translation services to clients worldwide. In this book, she shares her decades-long experience in remote work, beginning with her work as a freelancer in Port-au-Prince, Miami, Santa Cruz de la Sierra, Bolivia, and eventually starting her own company.

Becca is a writer and editor who works from a home office in the San Francisco Bay Area. She is an expert in cultivating camaraderie, agility, and collaboration within her online team. In *Your Work From Home Life*, she shares powerful advice gleaned from professional experience. Originally from Ohio, Becca credits her first-grade teacher as a great inspiration and runs several popular online classes and workshops.

Whatever your circumstances, you'll find nuggets of hard-earned wisdom in this book, along with hacks, how-tos, and advice from other teleworkers and experts.

We wish you prosperity in your work from home ventures!

M.J. Fievre and Becca Anderson

THE RULES OF ENGAGEMENT

I. Know What You're Signing Up For

II. Create Your Workspace

III. Know Your Peak Hours

IV. Understand the Basics of Planning and Scheduling

V. Set Boundaries Between Home and Work When Work Is at Home

VI. Stay Connected

VII. Practice Self-Care

VIII. Work on Your Career, Your Finances, and Yourself

IX. Know When to Ask for Help

X. Don't Forget about Gratitude

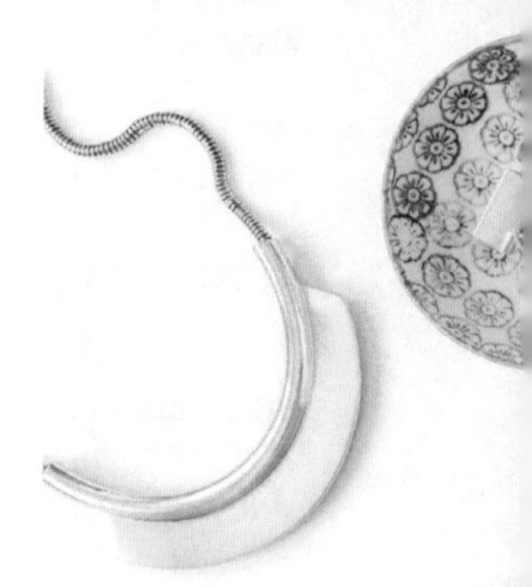

esc
tab
caps lock
shift
fn
control

CHAPTER 1

KNOW WHAT YOU'RE SIGNING UP FOR

While working from your couch sounds great in theory, it's important to understand the pros and cons so you know how to best optimize your arrangement. A pro of working from home may be that you can lounge in your sweatpants and stretch out with no one to notice the cookie crumbs on your keyboard, but the temptation to tap the "on" button on the television remote can be distracting, and, come summertime, if the kids are home during the day, it can become a challenge to focus on anything above the din of temper tantrums and calls for your immediate attention. Working from home is no less challenging than working from an office. It's all "work," after all. Keep the right mindset—knowing you may be putting in *more* effort than before.

THE PROS AND CONS OF WORKING REMOTELY

PROS

- ✓ True independence—you learn to rely on self-motivation, self-discipline, focus, and concentration. You may also have the ability to work anywhere.
- ✓ Flexible hours and increased productivity—you can get more work done, with the opportunity to learn new skills.
- ✓ No commute, which translates to huge savings in time and reduced work-related expenses (including gas and expensive clothes). When you can avoid a lengthy commute by car, train, or bus, it enables you to start your workday earlier and more calmly.
- ✓ A better work-life balance, with reduced stress and better health. Remote workers may have more time to incorporate physical exercise into their day.
- ✓ Better communication skills—out of necessity, you become very savvy in texting, emailing, and web meetings.

CONS

- ✕ Limited communication—technology makes it easy to interact with coworkers and clients, but it's not the same as face-to-face meetings, lunching together, or just engaging in everyday banter. No more regular happy hour with your coworkers at the end of a long day!
- ✕ Isolation and/or loneliness—it's hard to stay in the loop. Out of sight, out of mind. This may also lead to limited advancement and lower pay, since there's a danger of being overlooked for promotions or career development opportunities. People might wonder if you're taking it easy rather than pulling your own weight.
- ✕ Mental and physical exhaustion due to a lack of discipline. Many remote workers forget to clock out. During the workday, there may be too many—or not enough—distractions.
- ✕ Technological issues—you might not have full access to technology platforms. There may also be important cybersecurity issues that become your responsibility when you don't have the security of a workplace network and in-house IT department to rely on.

YOUR PROS AND CONS

Another of the pros of working from home is individualization. You can better adapt your working environment and functional role to your specific situation. In order to best do that, we suggest journaling about your current situation and finding your own specific pros and cons. If you are already working from home, you probably are already aware of your specific issues, but it's good practice to lay them out in writing so you can easily see what you'd like to achieve in terms of remodeling your career. If you're brand-new to the work from home lifestyle, now is a good time to project what you see moving forward.

Write a list of other benefits and challenges that may apply to your own situation. Be specific with the details, and write down any that come to mind.

Pros	Cons

Pros	Cons

QUESTIONS TO ASK YOUR EMPLOYER

Not only is your situation at home specific, your employer will also have their own specific needs and expectations. Policy and protocol between employers can vary widely from company to company, and you need to know how your employer prefers operational matters be handled. Here are some questions[1] you can have in mind during the hiring and orientation process to get you started on the right foot, so you can advance in your career with as few missteps as possible:

- **Schedule and Routine.** Who will I report to, and how often am I required to check in? How many hours are typically worked in a week? What is the expected schedule for online availability? What can I expect the day-to-day to look like? What are the expectations around working overtime? If the company is based in a different time zone, do I need to start later or earlier to match their time? Or do I work on the normal schedule within my time zone instead? What are the busiest times of year for the company?
- **Technology and Equipment.** What collaboration and workflow tools does the team use? What equipment, systems, and/or apps will I

need to perform the role remotely? Will you provide training, and, if so, how is that delivered? Do you provide general IT support for remote team members? If there is a budget for me to improve my home office, what is it, and how often is it renewed? Is there a loan agreement? Who will pay for return shipping or disposal of outdated equipment?

- **Team and Communication.** Can you tell me about the team I'll be working with? How often will I be in contact with other team members, and how many of them are remote? What methods do you use to keep people connected and enable collaboration? How often can team members come to and work out of the office if they are remote? Do you plan meetups for remote team members, or other ways to socialize? Does the company have company meetings or retreats where everyone is on-site? Am I required to visit the office or travel to other locations? How does working remotely enable the team to achieve its goals? Has it posed any challenges? How do you build team spirit?
- **Expectations.** What do you hope to see me accomplish in the first six months? How about within the first year? What can I do right away to hit the ground running?
- **Professional Development.** How will you measure my success? How do you see the responsibilities of my remote position changing over the next three years? What are the company's plans for

growth? What are the prospects for growth in my role? Do you offer continuing education and training? What types of support or learning encouragement does the company offer? Is there a budget for courses and books or for tuition reimbursement? Does the company provide any help for attending conferences?

- **Company Culture.** What are the main issues the company is facing right now? What about the major challenges a remote worker will face? What are some big-picture goals for the company in the coming year? What about in the next five years? How will my remote work contribute to the mission of the organization as a whole?

ADDITIONAL QUESTIONS

Brainstorm some additional questions that may apply to your own situation. Whether it's about reimbursement for childcare expenses or whether you can work remotely from an international location, don't be afraid to ask. Take a few minutes to jot down questions you think are relevant to you.

QUESTIONS TO ASK YOURSELF

It's important for you to understand what motives are driving you, and where you think you might face challenges moving forward. There may be some questions you hadn't considered[2] when opting for remote work. Here are some of the questions we think you need to have answered as you embark on or continue your career as a telecommuter. Don't worry if you don't have all the answers right this minute—much of this is information we cover in the book, and by the time you're done reading, you should have a better understanding of what works for you:

- **Motivation and Expectations.** Why are you choosing to work remotely? Do you have prior experience working remotely? What challenges do you think you'll face working remotely, and how will you deal with them? What's your favorite thing about working remotely? What's the highlight of your day? What is your most valuable asset when it comes to remote work? (That is, what do you bring to the table that would help you excel as a remote worker?) What are your goals for a month from now, three months from now? What do you hope to accomplish in the first six months? How about within the first year? What can you do right away to hit the ground running? What experience do you need to acquire for growth? How will your work contribute to the mission of your organization as a whole? What's the most challenging project you ever designed and executed?

- **Schedule and Routine.** What gets you up in the morning and motivates you to work? How do you handle your calendar and schedule? What apps/systems do you use? Do you have an open calendar everyone can see? What does your daily schedule look like? Your weekly schedule? Do you schedule blocks of time to do certain kinds of work? How do you organize files, links, and tabs on your computer? How do you prioritize tasks? What's most challenging for you in your daily work routine? How do you balance your work life and the rest of your life? What do you do when you sense a project is going to take longer than expected? How do you manage distractions during the day? Is it a challenge for you? How do you stay focused on your tasks? What tools have you used in the past to work effectively while remote? What do you need in your physical workspace to be successful in your job? What do you do to recharge each day? What activities do you do that help you maintain a work-life balance? Do you think you can fully disconnect at the end of the day or when you're on vacation? How do you switch off from work?
- **Setup, Technology, and Equipment.** What does "working remotely" look like for you? What's your setup like for working? Where do you prefer to work? What's one thing that would make your work easier

or better? What equipment, systems, and/or apps would help you perform better? How can you get training? Do you have a budget for new technology—or can you wait a little while? What about a budget to improve your home office? Can you afford a loan? How do you use different communication tools in different situations? How would you rate your tech skills? How do you use technology throughout the day, in your job and for pleasure? How would you manage a project with a lot of steps and a lot of people?

- **Team and Communication.** Do you know who all your team members are? How well do you feel you know your coworkers? How often are you in contact with them, and what are their preferred methods to stay connected? Which of your coworkers do you wish you had more of a connection with? How do you think that would help? Are some of them interested in socializing outside of work? How do you build team spirit? What helps you feel connected to others and counteract the potential loneliness of working remotely? What aspect of your team/the company do you want to learn more about? When you have a creative idea or epiphany, what do you do with it? Do you feel you have opportunities for "water-cooler" discussions with the team to help you generate ideas? Do you feel supported by the team such that you could go to anyone to ask for help? Do you feel included in team decisions? Why/why not? Do you feel the company supports remote staff effectively? What could be improved? What challenges do you feel you have, compared to those in the office? How do you prepare for meetings and facilitate meetings? What do you make sure to do during a meeting? How do you plan on communicating with a remote team? Think about an instance when you had to respond to a problem due to a communication failure. How would you handle lack of face-to-face contact when working remotely? If you had a problem when the rest of your remote team was offline, how would you go about solving it? How do you prefer to communicate with team members? What's your experience in working with distributed teams across time zones?

- **Professional Development.** How will you measure your own success? How do you see the responsibilities of your position changing over the next three years? What are your plans for growth? What are the prospects for growth in your role? Have you looked into continuing education and training?

ADDITIONAL QUESTIONS

You may have specific goals in mind for your future. Maybe you'd like to move to a different part of the country or world and want to know how state tax laws or international regulations differ from the region you're in now. Take a few minutes to sort those out, so you have a list you can work with over the next few weeks. Brainstorm some additional questions that may apply to your own situation.

TEAMS: THE WHO'S WHO CHECKLIST

It's important to know all the people on your team, what they do, how you can help each other, and how to get in touch with them. In the event of a technology failure, it's a good idea to have a handy list printed out with the following information for each member of your team, as well as having one stored on your computer for easy access.

- Name
- Official title
- Will help with
- Contact info

If you've answered the questions listed in this chapter and have set up a directory of team members, you're well on your way to a successful start at your new job! Understanding your motivations and the challenges and expectations for working remotely will help keep you motivated and on task. Understanding your employer's needs will help you better meet their expectations of you. It's important that your employer understand any needs you may have for things that will help you be more successful in completing your work. And it's important to realize that, even if you are working from home by yourself, you're not necessarily working alone. You have a team of people who rely on you to pull your own weight and show up virtually each day to help keep the workflow operating smoothly and efficiently. You will have a better chance of success if you put in the extra effort of staying connected and developing relationships with each member of your team, no matter how minimal your contact with them. Putting in the effort to learn the culture of your new job before you get started will help you prevent miscommunication and easily avoided mistakes.

FINDING REMOTE OPPORTUNITIES

Whether you're searching for the best remote jobs in order to unlock a more flexible schedule or want to land the kind of telework that'll empower you to travel the world, make sure to keep track of all your findings. The following worksheets will help guide your research.

Top Remote Jobs and Industries (Google it!)

Website	Link	Description	Notes

Online Certification Programs I Might Be Interested In **(Google it!)**

Website	Link	Description	Notes

Best Sites for Finding Remote Work Online: Remote-Only Job Boards **(Google it!)**

Website	Link	Description	Notes

Worst Sites for Finding Remote Work Online: Remote-Only Job Boards (Google it!)

Website	Link	Description	Notes

Remote Companies That Offer Flexible Schedules, High Pay, and Creative Work (Google it!)

Website	Link	Description	Notes

General Interest Job Sites **(Google it!)**

Website	Link	Description	Notes

Create Your Own Checklist: Tips for Writing a Remote Work Resume **(Google it!)**

Website	Link	Description	Notes

Facebook Groups Focused on Remote Work **(Facebook it!)**

Website	Link	Description	Notes

Blogging Opportunities **(Google it!)**

Website	Link	Description	Notes

CHAPTER 2

CREATE YOUR WORKSPACE

Not everyone has the luxury of working out of their home alone. Many people have pets, children, roommates, partners or spouses, noisy or intrusive neighbors, and constant interruptions—from a ringing doorbell to construction in the neighborhood—to manage in a typical day. It can get chaotic. Even if there isn't enough room for you to set a whole room aside for office space, you'll find it's easier to avoid distractions with a dedicated workspace that can ensure you the privacy you need to focus. If you don't already have a home office, pick a spot that can be yours indefinitely, and make that your dedicated space. Declare that it is off-limits when you are working from home, except for emergencies. It's a good idea to stay away from spaces that are associated with leisure time, such as your bedroom or the couch. Think of this space as your work "sanctuary." Keep this "desk" clean, neat, and organized. At the end of each workday, clear the clutter.

That way, you will feel energized when you sit down at your desk the next day.

TIPS TO SET UP YOUR WORKSPACE[3]

- **Ensure your home office is a dedicated and private space.** We know this can be a tough challenge: Find the best location, consider who else uses the space, and have a productive conversation about work needs, compromise, and privacy. Work in an environment that matches your auditory sweet spot (some prefer silence, others like background music or white noise), a place that is organized, free of distractions, and comfortable.
- **Get the equipment you need.** Make sure you have all the tools and resources required to complete your work readily available and at hand. If you're employed by a company or organization that supports your work from home setup, request the equipment you need to get your job done comfortably, including the right computer and monitor, keyboard, mouse, chair, printer or multipurpose machine, software, and so forth. You'll need high-speed internet access. Consider a room divider. You might also need a telephone and/or VoIP, a network router, a surge protector,

and an uninterruptible power supply (UPS). Research the right equipment for your ergonomic home office; your Google search will list elements such as laptop riser, external keyboard, external mouse, cushions and pillows, rolled-up towel, orthopedic seat, footrest, voice dictation software, microphone, white-noise machine, and lamp.

- **Incorporate your own style.** Making design decisions about your workspace improves productivity as well as health and happiness. Even if your dedicated workspace is just a corner off the kitchen, if it's pleasant to look at and comfortable, you're more likely to want to work in that space than if it's dull and lacking any personality.
- **Apply principles of feng shui,** a practice that applies spatial arrangement and energy balance for optimum design and layout. Look up where to position your desk, for instance. And use a color that improves your productivity; in feng shui, green is associated with growth and decisiveness. Include natural light and proper lighting; natural light increases your energy levels, helps you focus, and reduces stress. Improve your home office's air quality. Set the right temperature, too; productivity decreases when you're either too hot or too cold. While there are several factors to consider, keeping the temperature between 70 and 72 degrees (21–22°C) is usually ideal.
- **Choose comfort.** Make sure to get the right desk and a chair with proper lumbar support. (Google "ergonomic chair.") Incorporate

a standing desk too, so you can alternate standing with sitting throughout the day. Don't forget to help out your neck and eyes, too. Make sure you've got your monitor in the "perfect" spot.

- **Clear your home office of clutter.** Stash it away: Less is more. Remember to tame the wires. Clutter creates a kind of chaos all its own, and an organized workspace saves times searching through piles for important items you need to find quickly.
- **Protect sensitive or important documents.** You may need a backup drive or personal server, a file cabinet, and a fire-safe box.

BEST COLORS FOR PRODUCTIVITY

Science has shown that humans associate colors with specific moods, and that colors influence our physical and mental/emotional states. Some colors are stimulating, some are calming. Does the color scheme of your new workspace reflect your needs? The following handy list[4] will help you see what color schemes can do for your mood and productivity level, and help you select a palette that's right for you.

Color	Description	Associated with	Where to Use
Blue	intellectual, soothing, helps calm the mind and aids concentration, enhances wakefulness and supports clear communication	trust, logic, communication, and efficiency	office areas that require maximum focus and mental rigor
Green	restful, balanced, creates a sense of calm and reassurance, provides a productivity boost	harmony, nature, and restoration	offices that require people to work long hours; offices where a sense of balance is top priority (including medical, yoga, or a meditative practice)
Red	physical, stimulating, active, intense, and alarming at times; gets the heart pumping and raises the pulse, activates the "fight or flight" instinct	courage, strength, and excitement	areas of the workplace that demand physical exertion

Color	Description	Associated with	Where to Use
Yellow	emotional, energizing, fresh, radiates positivity, stimulates creativity	creativity, friendliness, optimism, and confidence	workplaces that need to stimulate positivity, creativity, and happiness; work environments where creative professionals, such as artists, writers, designers, and developers work
Purple	spiritual	spirituality or luxury (with the opposite effect if not used carefully)	workplaces that promote deep contemplation or luxury
Orange	blends the physical (red) and emotional (yellow), creating a sense of comfort	food and warmth, fun	casual office lounges
Grey	neutral	neutrality (lack of confidence if used inappropriately)	sleek or modern offices

THE ESSENTIAL LIST OF OFFICE SUPPLIES FOR YOUR HOME OFFICE

To create a streamlined and efficient home office, think about the essentials you'll need to get your work done. From paper clips to a stress ball, don't leave anything out. Use the space below to help you figure out the items you'll need in your home office, depending on the type of work you do and how much space you have available.

For My Desktop and Desk Drawers

Paper and Stationery Supplies

Filing and Storage Supplies

Calendar and Planning Supplies

Short List of Equipment

Decor

Free printable lists are available online to help you create your own.[5]

THE DOCUMENTS CHECKLIST

Organizing your home office includes keeping it free of paper clutter. Here's a checklist to organize your hanging files and manila folders.

- **Vital Documents:** adoption records, birth certificates, passports, marriage certificates, divorce decrees, death certificates, driver's licenses, Social Security cards, immigration papers, household inventory, insurance information (by type), legal records, military records, power of attorney documents, religious records, safe-deposit box inventories, living wills
- **Finances:** bank statements, voided/deposited checks, loan information (including student loans), closed accounts, checking, savings, credit card information, credit card statements, mortgages, real estate records, credit reports, utilities/monthly bills (electricity, water, cable, cell phone, internet), insurance information and payments (by type), investment accounts, 401k, IRA, Social Security, mutual funds, stocks, pension, charity, tax documents (including donations, expenses/receipts, and paystubs), warranties, household expenses

- **Education, Career, Income:** transcripts and other educational records, degrees, diplomas, resume, employment information, pay stubs, offer letters, W4, benefit summaries
- **Vehicle Information:** maintenance, insurance, title/lease, registration
- **Medical Documents:** medical records (by person), health insurance, statements, bills to be submitted, bills submitted (not paid), bills paid, receipts, HSA healthcare expenses
- **Lifestyle:** childcare, clubs, dog training, family history, health/vitamins/diet, hobbies, holidays, home decorating, humor, landscape ideas, maps, grocery lists, takeout and restaurant menus, schedules, travel and vacation ideas, volunteer work, wish list, uniforms

YOUR HANGING FILE ORGANIZER

Use this worksheet to organize your files before you put them in manila folders.

CATEGORY:

FILES: ______________________

____

____

____

CATEGORY:

FILES: ______________________

____

____

____

THE PASSWORD ORGANIZER

There are online programs you can use to organize your passwords, but it's also smart to keep a printed list handy in case you are working away from home or need it for some other reason. Remember to use a different password for each account you need to log into, and make them complex and hard to crack to deter hackers who could compromise your important accounts and exploit your private information. You can use the following template as a guideline to help you set up your own password organizer.

Website:		**Website:**	
USERNAME	______________	**USERNAME**	______________
PASSWORD	______________	**PASSWORD**	______________
EMAIL USED	______________	**EMAIL USED**	______________
SECURITY ANSWER	______________	**SECURITY ANSWER**	______________
MISC. NOTES		**MISC. NOTES**	

SETTING UP YOUR VIRTUAL OFFICE: THE LIST OF ESSENTIAL APPS

The internet has a wealth of handy tools[6] to help you with various facets of your work and home life. Here are some that we recommend:

1. **Focus:** Using the Pomodoro technique, Be Focused (available on your Mac) keeps track of your tasks and will interrupt you at regular intervals to make sure you're taking your needed breaks to rest. Focus Keeper (for iPhone and iPad) also uses the Pomodoro technique; Daywise schedules notifications to stop work and reminds you to take some free time. Ambient Noise is great for concentration. Serene is another tool that cuts out distractions, helping you stay focused and complete tasks faster.
2. **Time Management:** Toggl keeps track of how long it's really taking you to complete tasks. Zapier saves you time on repetitive tasks and switching between apps by automating processes (e.g., automatically saving Gmail attachments to Google Drive). Create your to-do list with Evernote. The app also allows you to

jot down notes, take photos, make voice recordings, or otherwise preserve your ideas for future use (before they slip your mind).

3. **Email Solutions:** Spark is a smart email client that stops your inbox from getting in the way of productivity and turns it into an asset. Inboxcube sorts your emails in cubes so it's easier to hunt for a particular message.
4. **Scheduling:** Use Doodle to set up meetings. Google Calendar also helps you manage all your calendars and events in one place and arrange meetings without exchanging dozens of emails.
5. **File Creation and Sharing:** Microsoft Office (including Word, Excel, PowerPoint, and Outlook) is still the productivity software chosen by many businesses. Alternatively, Apple's Pages creates rich text documents. Chrome Remote Desktop allows you to access your computer securely from any device and screen-share with teammates for stronger collaboration. Google Drive allows for document creation, cloud storage, file sharing, and collaboration. You and your coworkers can work on the same document simultaneously to make sure all necessary voices are heard on projects. DropBox allows you to access your stored files from any device with an internet connection; you can also share collaborative folders. TeamViewer is a remote desktop

support tool that lets you connect to another computer over the internet and take control of it.

6. **Collaboration:** Asana is a full-featured, easy-to-use project management platform. Trello is one of the best apps to help you organize tasks and track your team members' progress. Check out Monday and Smartsheet as well.
7. **Communication:** Slack is a real-time communications tool that allows you to create topic-based channels, direct-message with coworkers, and make audio and video calls. Zoom offers video and voice calls for groups and one-to-one. Skype offers instant chat, calls, video chat, and SMS messaging—all from the same interface. Microsoft Teams is also a great resource.
8. **Finances:** Expensify is expense management software with a cloud-based app that allows you to easily record expenses, store scanned receipts, and submit reimbursement requests. We also like QuickBooks.
9. **Professional Networking:** The LinkedIn app helps you stay connected with colleagues, professionals in your field, and friends—an especially important feature for people who work from home, which can be isolating at times.

ESSENTIAL APPS: YOUR OWN RESEARCH

Search the internet for the types of remote work tools you'll need and decide which is the best in each category.

Type	Name	Recommended By
Focus apps		
Time-management tools		
To-do list apps		
Note-taking apps		
Online office suites		
Mobile hotspots		
Remote desktop software		
Cloud storage		
Email solutions		

Type	Name	Recommended By
Automation tools		
Security tools		
Scheduling apps		
Collaboration: File creation and sharing		
Collaboration: Project management software		
Whiteboard and mind-mapping tools		
Communication: Team chat apps		
Communication: Videoconferencing apps		
Communication: Screen-sharing software		
Communication: Screen recording tools		
Professional networking		
Financial tools		

STRATEGIC ORGANIZATION

Organization helps you sleep better; reduces your stress, depression, and anxiety; improves your relationships; frees up time and energy to improve your life in other areas; and helps you make better choices. Putting in the effort of getting organized, especially if this organization extends to multiple areas of your life, can help reduce stress levels long-term by requiring less last-minute scrambling in a variety of everyday situations.

Dr. Heidi Hanna, author of *Stressaholic*,[7] explains that the brain is constantly scanning the environment, looking for cues that signal a need for an energy investment, such as taking care of work or home obligations. When we have chaotic surroundings or a fragmented mindset, the brain can perceive this as a sign that there is more demand for energy than our current capacity, which triggers the stress response.

Strategic organization is helpful when we are able to prioritize in a thoughtful way, assuming it leads us to action. We suggest you make a master list of everything you need to do—yes, *everything*—and start crushing those tasks you've been avoiding. Organize your house, organize your time, and be proactive. Review your calendar and plan your schedule for the week; fill in your planner for next month. Create your morning and evening routines.

When getting organized, don't forget your electronics. Delete old contacts from your phone. Sort your photos and delete unwanted, unneeded, and duplicate pictures. Organize files on your phone and computer. Clean out your inbox: reply to all of your email—all of it! (Oh, the madness!) Review all your paid subscriptions and cancel accounts that you don't like anymore. Back up your computer, delete any unnecessary documents, and install a password encryption service on your laptop. Clean your keyboard and computer screen. Update your social media profiles and download useful apps on your phone.

You can be organized in your life in a host of ways. Give it a try and start feeling less stressed today.

THE HOME OFFICE DECLUTTERING CHECKLIST

"I hate housework. You make the beds, you wash the dishes, and six months later you have to start all over again." **—Joan Rivers**

Having a home office can keep you productive and professional, and separate your work life from your home life. A dedicated workspace can also help reduce distractions like social media. Paying attention to the design and setup of your home office is a smart business move, since it translates into greater comfort, increased productivity, and ultimately more income. When designed well and kept clean, your home office becomes a "silent partner," supporting your efforts and increasing your effectiveness.

How to Keep a Clean Home Office			
Every Day	Every Week	Every Month	Every Season
☺ Sort mail ☺ Straighten up	☺ Dust and vacuum ☺ Dust electronics	☺ Wipe computers ☺ File documents/ important papers	☺ Wash windows ☺ Clean blinds/ curtains ☺ Back up and/or delete old files on computer ☺ Refill office supplies

Remember as you are setting up your workspace that a little effort goes a long way in boosting your productivity and morale, and that your office space can be as unique as you are. If you're stuck for ideas on how to individualize your workspace, check out Pinterest for tips on managing specific space challenges. There are plenty of storage solutions available that will meet your needs and get you up and running. But more importantly than the initial setup, staying organized helps you stay focused for the long run. It only takes a little effort to do the few tasks you need to do to keep everything in order.

CHAPTER 3

KNOW YOUR PEAK HOURS...AND EAT THE FROG!

If you're ready to start working from home or have just made the leap into self-employment, here's one of the best time-management tips we have to offer: *Find your peak hours.*

When do you have the most energy? Adjust your schedule accordingly. *Do your heavy lifting when you're at your best.* For some, that means getting up early, before anyone else in the house is awake, and completing the most dreaded tasks first thing in the morning, tackling the *first item* on their list *first thing* in the morning. If you're a morning person, schedule the hardest tasks on your to-do list for before noon, when you know you'll be in the right headspace for them. If you're a night owl, you'll notice increased productivity when you work while the rest of the world slumbers. Give yourself tougher tasks to perform when you're at your peak. Use slower points of the day to knock out the easier, more logistical tasks that are also on your plate.

Find out your productive hours by listening to your body clock. In any case, eat the frog first.

Sounds disgusting, we know, but there's a lot of wisdom behind that statement. Imagine you have to eat a live frog; you might as well get it over with quickly. There's no point in dragging it out, putting it off, or staring at the frog on your plate. "Mark Twain once said that, if the first thing you do each morning is to eat a live frog, you can go through the day with the satisfaction of knowing that that is probably the worst thing that is going to happen to you all day long," writes Brian Tracy. "Your 'frog' is your biggest, most important task, the one you are most likely to procrastinate on if you don't do something about it." (Google "Brian Tracy" and "eat a frog.")

Brian Tracy suggests that we do the hardest or most important task first thing in our workday. Eat the frog! When you finally do it, you will feel so much better, ready to take on the rest of your day!

PEAK HOURS: THE "GETTING STARTED" ROUTINE FOR *YOUR WORK FROM HOME LIFE*

After you've figured out your peak hours, having a "getting started" routine[8] is like stretching before you sprint, but may be even more important because you're readying your brain as well as your body for a day of work. You can customize your routine to suit your specific needs. It will enable you to make the mental shift from relaxation time to workday, the same way that a commute to a traditional workplace allows you to get in the right mindset for a day at the office. If you're interested in establishing a great "getting started" routine, here are some ideas.

Be practical. Develop a "getting started" routine that works on weekends, too.

Start your routine the night before. Set up for the morning the night before, during your shut-down routine. It helps to not have to spend a lot of time on setup in the morning. After you've cleaned your workspace in the evening, make sure you have everything you need for the next day. Keep your working area tidy.

Set your hours for the next day. If your boss didn't set a schedule, create your own—and stick to it! By setting a deadline to complete your work each day, you will remain on track and avoid working over your allotted hours. If you work a little here, and a little there, an eight-hour day might stretch into a ten- or twelve-hour workday, and this leads to mental and physical exhaustion. It may be a good idea to structure your day as you would in the office and pick a definite finishing time each day. This will keep you from working too much or working too little, whichever is your tendency.

It's also a good idea to create a to-do list the night before—a tangible reminder of what you need to get done the next day. Prioritize the tasks on your to-do list ahead of time. Focus on result-oriented activities. Estimate how much time each item will take and assign a specific time to each one. Don't overestimate your abilities. Be realistic about what you can achieve, and then get to it!

To cut down your to-do list, ask yourself two questions: What are the important tasks on this list? How many of these important tasks can I realistically accomplish or make significant progress on tomorrow?

Keep it simple. Group similar tasks into a single batch. Move extra items to your "might-do list"—you can always move these items to the following day and yet "clock out" with a solid list of tasks filed under "complete."

Once your list has been created, create personal events and reminders on your online calendar (Google Calendar makes this easy) so you'll know when to shift gears and start on new tasks.

When you solidify your schedule the day before, it feels more official when you wake up the next day and get started on it.

The night before, remember to **disengage:** zero notifications from apps and phones at night.

Remember to **wake up at YOUR right time.** Some prefer to wake up early because they'll have more opportunity to get things done. Morning is generally a productive part of the day for most people, so

METHODS FOR SCHEDULING

Five-minute slots. How does Elon Musk run both Tesla and SpaceX? He breaks his entire day into five-minute slots—even his lunch. Doing so keeps him productive, since it ensures that he stays on track and doesn't waste his time.

"Must, Should, Want" method. Here's a simple exercise from Jay Shirley. When scheduling your day, answer three questions: What must you do to create the most impact today? What should you do to build a better future? What do you want to do so that you can enjoy today and life more completely?

the more of it, the better. Others prefer waking up late because they feel energized and motivated later in the day. In either case, don't snooze past your peak productivity time.

Focus on your body first. Drink some lemon water, and then start the day with exercise. Working out on an empty stomach is great for your body's energy levels and for burning fat. It also primes the brain for a productive day ahead. Aerobic exercise is particularly good for you. It will lift your mood and clear your mind for the day ahead. Eat a good breakfast (preferably one that is fast and easy). A nutritious breakfast will stabilize your eating habits during the day. Make sure you have enough protein, fiber, and healthy fats. Skip the coffee early in the morning. Coffee is

The Eisenhower Matrix. This strategy was developed by Dwight Eisenhower. Separate your tasks based on four possibilities: urgent and important (tasks you will do immediately); important, but not urgent (tasks you will schedule to do later); urgent, but not important (tasks you will delegate to someone else); neither urgent nor important (tasks you will eliminate).

The "big rocks" system based on the principles outlined by Stephen R. Covey, author of *The Seven Habits of Highly Effective People*. Schedule time for your most important priorities first by imagining them as "big rocks" filling a bucket or jar. If you start with "big rocks," and then put in sand or smaller rocks, all the gaps and cracks will get filled.

healthy, but you want to avoid having it when your cortisol levels peak early in the morning.

Then focus on your mind. We recommend meditation: you only need to meditate for twenty minutes a day to experience benefits. It helps you relax, and there many proven health benefits to meditation. Spending thirty minutes on a hobby or skill can be a good alternative to meditation.

Get dressed. One perk of working from home is that you can wear whatever you want. Beware! If you look and feel sloppy, it can cause you to be disorganized in your thoughts—and your work as well. Pretend you are going to the office and establish a "getting started" routine that includes getting up and preparing for the day. Take a shower and put on something professional (yet comfortable)—it's a key step in helping you mentally transition into work mode.

Eat the frog! Focus on one task at a time. Do not multitask. And no screen time until you've eaten the frog! After completing the most important task on your to-do list, focus your attention on those that fall under the "two-minute rule." According to David Allen, author of the bestselling *Getting Things Done*,[9] if a task takes under two minutes to complete, do it now—so it's out of the way. Get that easy win! While you should usually focus on tackling the hardest tasks first, sometimes you need an instant victory, like making your bed when you wake up. It's a simple way to feel accomplished and build momentum for the rest of the day. It's also a good idea to start with solitary tasks in the morning. This will give you time to become productive. Save phone calls, meetings, and other collaborative work for when you've officially "woken up" and found your groove.

Be optimistic. Give yourself something nice to look at. Listen to music that boosts productivity. Find meaning in what you do (and love what you do). Set some exciting goals and tell other people about them. Be proactive, not reactive. Give up on the illusion of perfection and reward yourself for finishing a big task; it is an effective way to keep you motivated and productive. Own your mistakes, then move on. We all make mistakes; learn from them so you won't repeat them in the future. Develop a growth mindset: according to Stanford psychologist Carol Dweck, those with a growth mindset "believe that their most basic abilities can be developed through dedication and hard work—brains and talent are just the starting point. This view creates a love of learning and a resilience that is essential for great accomplishment."

CHECKLIST—PEAK HOURS: THE "GETTING STARTED" ROUTINE FOR YOUR WORK FROM HOME LIFE

1. Be practical.
2. Start your routine the night before.
3. Remember to disengage at night.
4. Wake up at your right time.
5. Focus on your body first.
6. Then focus on your mind.
7. Get dressed.
8. Eat the frog!
9. Be optimistic.

THE END-OF-DAY ROUTINE

Avoid randomness. Working from home can be a convenience, but it can create stress if there's no separation between your workday and your leisure time. Without a clear separation of parts of your day, your workday can bleed over into your leisure time and make you feel like your life is all about work. It's best to set clear boundaries so you have time to recharge and rejuvenate your mind and body. Take control of your "end of day" routine[10]—it will make you feel more relaxed, peaceful and happy.

Create a habit that signals the close of the workday. Something as simple as shutting down your computer and turning on *Golden Girls* or *Family Guy* will do. Whatever you choose, do it consistently to mark the end of working hours.

1. **Decide when the workday ends.** Set a specific time to completely **check out from work** so you can recharge your batteries. Doing so ensures you'll be fully energized the following day.
2. **Take time to tidy.** When you have a cluttered desk, it sends a visual cue to your brain that causes stress. Spend the last couple

of minutes of your day cleaning and organizing your desk so it's clear for the next day.

3. Prepare for tomorrow. **Plan out the next day.**

   "Failing to plan is planning to fail." **—Benjamin Franklin**

   "The best preparation for tomorrow is doing your best today." **—H. Jackson Brown, Jr.**

   "Read Goals Before Sleeping. Review your goals twice every day in order to be focused on achieving them." **—Les Brown**

4. **Give yourself time to decompress from your day,** but don't wind down with your gadgets. Create a no-phone zone and step away from the screens. This will protect you from the negativity of others. (Blue wavelengths from fluorescent lights and electronic devices can also fatigue your eyes and accelerate eye aging.)

   "Protect your enthusiasm from the negativity of others." **—H. Jackson Brown, Jr.**

5. **Set an exclusive family ritual routine.** Play a family game or watch a favorite show together.

   "The bond that links your true family is not one of blood, but of respect and joy in each other's life." **—Richard Bach**

6. **Do one thing you love.** For instance, read a book. Or unleash your imagination.

"A hobby a day keeps the doldrums away."—**Phyllis McGinley**

"Imagination is the beginning of creation. You imagine what you desire, you will what you imagine, and at last you create what you will."—**George Bernard Shaw**

7. **Write in your happiness journal.** Reflect on your day and put things in perspective, acknowledging your wins. Ending your day on a high note encourages you to do the same the next day. Give some gratitude. As explained in *Daring to Live Fully*, "When you take a moment to remember a positive experience, your brain labels it as meaningful, which deepens the imprint."

   "When it comes to life, the critical thing is whether you take things for granted or take them with gratitude."—**Gilbert K. Chesterton**

8. **Say your Personal Evening Conviction.**

   "It's the repetition of affirmations that leads to belief. And once that belief becomes a deep conviction, things begin to happen."
   —Muhammad Ali

9. **Practice self-care.** Do some bedtime yoga, stretch to release tension, or try a sleep meditation. Take care of hygiene rituals. Take a warm bath two to three hours before bed. Have a healthy dinner, and if you're hungry again, eat a light, pre-bedtime snack. Get rid of caffeine after four o'clock and stay hydrated. In order to get a quality night's rest, also avoid alcohol for several hours before you hit the hay.

10. **Go to bed at the same time every night.** Getting seven to nine hours of quality sleep every night improves your attention, concentration, creativity, decision-making, and health. It also reduces stress and impulsiveness. Don't get into bed until right before it's time to sleep. Make your bed an oasis.

CHECKLIST—THE END-OF-DAY ROUTINE

1. Decide when the workday ends.
2. Take time to tidy.
3. Plan out the next day.
4. Give yourself time to decompress from your day.
5. Set an exclusive family ritual routine.
6. Do one thing you love.
7. Write in your happiness journal.
8. Say your Personal Evening Conviction.
9. Practice self-care.
10. Go to bed at the same time every night.

TAKE A BREAK

Plan for breaks. It may seem counterintuitive, but you'll maximize productivity by taking mini breaks throughout the day. In order to stay organized, try to take your breaks at the same times each day. Some people use laundry as a work timer: Start and finish something from your to-do list during the wash cycle—and take a break before changing the load. Or set an alarm. It's important to step away from the computer now and then to recharge, refuel, and refocus. Make a sandwich. Play with your cat. Take a walk in the backyard. It's a good idea to break up work periods with exercise. Just breathe.

Don't shortchange yourself during breaks, especially your lunch hour. You can use an app to lock yourself out of your computer. Or you can just launch a simple clock or timer on the screen when you take a break. "There's a lot to be said about the power of rest throughout the workday," writes Renzo Costarella. "If you power through the day without taking the time to decompress, you'll do yourself more harm than good.... The best way to take breaks is to schedule them throughout your day. That way you can truly control the flow of work."

Sometimes you need to completely unplug and disconnect in order to recharge and avoid burnout. On your days off, it might be a good idea to shut off your phone for a couple of hours so that you aren't answering phone calls, texts, or emails.

Take time for yourself and do whatever (healthy) thing recharges and refreshes you. Get enough sleep. (Google "polyphasic sleep schedule.") Eat a healthy diet. Drink lots of water. The healthier you are, the more productive you'll be. And the more productive you are with your work, the more time you'll have to spend however you like. Get rid of your bad habits, whether it's smoking or hanging around toxic people. Hold standing meetings to avoid sitting for too long. Organize your office to keep your sanity.

TAKE A BREAK: THE BASIC RULES

1. **Establish break triggers:** Pay attention to the signals your body sends you that lets you know it's time to step away from your workload for a break. If you find your mind wandering, for example, it might be a signal that you need to step outside and

stretch for ten minutes or take a short meditation break.

2. **Plan your breaks in advance:** Set up a routine for yourself that allows you to take scheduled breaks throughout the day, even if it is just to make a cup of tea or close your eyes for five minutes.
3. **Don't be too hard on yourself:** You may find that some days it's harder to focus than others. Give yourself a break.

THREE SCIENTIFIC REASONS TO PRIORITIZE BREAKS AT WORK

1. Breaks keep us from getting bored (and thus, unfocused)
2. Breaks help us retain information and make connections
3. Breaks help us reevaluate our goals

TAKE A BREAK: SEVEN BREAK METHODS TO TRY[11]

1. **The Pomodoro method.** One of the most common ways to implement a schedule with breaks—especially when you're busy—is to work in short bursts, typically twenty-five minutes, followed by a three-to-four-minute break and a fifteen-to-thirty-minute break after four intervals. This method typically involves a timer to make sure you are taking time out. (Google it!)
2. **Sixty-minute work blocks.** One hour of uninterrupted work time yields the equivalent of three hours of work in a normal work environment. The keyword is "uninterrupted."
3. **The 52-17 model** using the app DeskTime. (Google "52-17" and "DeskTime.")
4. **Two fifteen-minute breaks** per day, in addition to an hour break—which is what most jobs allow.
5. **A break every twenty minutes.** Alan Hedge (an ergonomics expert and a professor emeritus at Cornell University) says that a break about once every twenty minutes prevents computer-work-related injuries.

6. **12 percent.** A study found that the optimal amount of time for breaks is about 12 percent of the workday. Applied to an eight-hour workday, that's about fifty-eight minutes of break time. As an example, five breaks of about twelve minutes each would do the trick.
7. **Follow your ultradian rhythms**—the natural rhythms that the body cycles through every 90 to 120 minutes. The idea is that you should concentrate when your energy levels are highest, but rest when you feel drained.

SIGNS THAT YOU SHOULD TAKE A BREAK[12]

- **Lack of energy:** If it feels like you've lost your oomph, it's a good idea to find a way to get it back. Often it just means you need to take a breather, get something to eat, and refocus.
- **Lack of motivation:** It's hard to work if you've lost interest in the task at hand. Try taking a few minutes to listen to some upbeat music to get your motivation back on track.

- **More frequent frustration:** Trying to work through frustration can just lead to more frustration and to feelings of being overwhelmed. Take some deep breaths and relax when you feel like your fuse is short.
- **Feeling fuzzy headed:** You're more likely to make mistakes if your thinking is muddled. Take time away from the desk if you can't keep on task. Come back to the task when your thinking is clear and your mind is sharp again.
- **Mild health issues:** If you find that you've got a nagging cramp in your neck that won't go away, or aches and pains that have no clear cause, it might be that you're not taking enough time for yourself during the day. Listen to your body!
- **Sleep disturbances due to stress:** Plagued by nightmares that leave you tossing and turning till dawn? It's a good sign you need to relax and manage your stress level better. Taking more frequent breaks is a good way to ensure you aren't overloading yourself.

THREE THINGS THAT HELP YOU FEEL RECHARGED[13]

---

1. Positive work reflection (thinking and talking about the positive aspects of your job)
2. Mastery (working on a skill)
3. Relaxation

THINGS TO DO DURING YOUR BREAK[14]

1. **Relax and laugh.** According to *A Life of Productivity,* smiling makes you more productive because it boosts your immunity, makes you happier and more able to handle stress, and helps you focus on the big picture. There are plenty of reasons to smile: Sit back and daydream. Meditate. Read a nonwork book. Doodle or paint a Picasso-worthy work of art. Pick a new desktop background. Watch funny cat videos on YouTube. Get lost in Buzzfeed. Head over to The Oatmeal and laugh at some quality online comics. Listen to your favorite music or create your ultimate work playlist to help you power through the rest of the day. Stressed about something? Scream into the void (screamintothevoid.com/) and watch it fade into the stars.
2. **Change your mood.** Use brainwave entrainment to influence your brainwave patterns and help change your state of mind. Stop and smell the…lemons: "Research from the Ohio State University found that sniffing lemon improved people's moods and raised levels of norepinephrine, a brain chemical linked to executive decision-making and motivation. Another study

found that students exposed to a citrus-scented cleaner were more likely to clean up after themselves, while in a Japanese study the scent of lemon improved typing accuracy, with workers making 54 percent fewer errors." Or pay attention to your best friend: Play with your dog! Studies have found that we "become more trusting, relaxed and nicer" after interacting with a canine. Furthermore, playing with your best friend reduces stress.

3. **Feed your imagination.** One of the best ways to boost your imagination and creativity is to brainstorm: Browse *National Geographic's* photography archives. Plan a staycation or something fun. Create your bucket list: check out BucketList.net, Life'd's ultimate bucket list, and Tumblr's bucket list tags. Write a blog post or create lists. Make a procrastination list—a list of high-leverage activities that you can chip away at whenever you're procrastinating or have downtime. (Examples include reading industry magazines, organizing folders, or reviewing your contact lists.) You may also choose to create a stop-doing list—a list of those bad habits that waste your time or hinder your productivity. Write these habits down and develop a realistic plan to replace these bad habits with good habits. What about a list of your keystone habits? Charles Duhigg, author of *The Power of Habit*, defines "keystone habits" as those that can transform your life. Examples include planning out your days, exercising, and having strong willpower.

4. **Fuel your inspiration and motivation.** Use the power of visualization. "Mental practice can get you closer to where you want to be in life, and it can prepare you for success!" writes A.J. Adams, MAPP, in *Psychology Today*. For example, in a study of weight trainers, those "who carried out virtual workouts in their heads" increased muscle strength by almost half again as much when compared to those who didn't. Find some inspiring stories online to get you motivated and excited. Many TED talks will get you revved up to do just about anything. Spend some time on Pinterest and create a board to inspire your career. Instead of a to-do list, create a "done list" where you write down everything you've already accomplished. It's a powerful way to keep you motivated when you need a boost.
5. **Care for your body.** Move! Do some desk stretches to reverse that computer hunch. You can achieve twice as much by keeping fit because exercise keeps the brain functioning well: walk two laps around your block or building—or walk up and down a few flights of stairs. Grab some brain-boosting snacks; avoid sugar, simple carbohydrates like pasta and bread, and junk food—they can give you a temporary energy high, but then you may crash. Make yourself a coffee. (Use caffeine strategically: It can take about twenty minutes for a cup of coffee to kick in, so drink it twenty minutes before you need to power up.) Recharge by taking a quick nap, preferably in the afternoon; you'll feel much

more awake and ready to get back to the grind, as napping can improve your memory, alertness, and creativity. Sometimes, it might be enough to simply strike a power pose, which tells your brain, "I'm in control." According to Murray Newlands, "having a power pose in place for around two minutes may assist with confidence, decrease stress, and encourage a greater tolerance for risk." (Google Murray's seven body positions.)

6. **Spread some cheer.** Call a loved one. (Make the phone call while walking back and forth; the combination of movement and chatting will provide a boost of energy before you head back to your desk. Remember to focus on the conversation at hand, however, to avoid misunderstandings.) Send a coworker a funny e-card. Or send a thank-you note to someone who's helped you out recently.
7. **Organize.** Clear out your home office drawers, rearrange your files, organize your smartphone, and update your online passwords using a tool like 1Password, PassPack, or Password Genie. Consolidate your tools and apps—limit yourself to the essentials. Unsubscribe from ten email newsletters.
8. **Network.** See what your Facebook or LinkedIn contacts have been up to and send some congratulatory emails. Follow LinkedIn influencers to soak up career wisdom from people who

have had major success themselves. While you're there, spruce up your own profile.

9. **Do nothing.** The website donothingfor2minutes.com forces you to sit, relax, and gaze at a beautiful photo to really clear your head. The second you move your mouse, you have to start all over.

CHECKLIST—THINGS TO DO DURING YOUR BREAK

- ☐ Relax and laugh.
- ☐ Change your mood.
- ☐ Feed your imagination.
- ☐ Fuel your inspiration and motivation.
- ☐ Care for your body.
- ☐ Spread some cheer.
- ☐ Organize.
- ☐ Network.
- ☐ Do nothing.

LEARN SOMETHING NEW

"The key to pursuing excellence is to embrace an organic, long-term learning process, and not to live in a shell of static, safe mediocrity. Usually, growth comes at the expense of previous comfort or safety."

—Josh Waitzkin, American chess player, martial arts competitor, and author

Researchers tell us that one of the best things we can do to protect ourselves from certain types of dementia is to flex our mental muscles. This includes using our brains in new ways and continually challenging ourselves to learn new things.

While you're at home, enrich your general knowledge and surf the internet to know more about some interesting topics or facts. Read online newspapers. Learn a new skill by watching tutorials on YouTube or binge on a documentary about someone truly fabulous. Listen to a new podcast or audiobook. Create a to-read book list. Sign up for a virtual class or watch useful tutorials. Visit an online exhibit. Get lost on Quora and read about conspiracy theories.

Learning a new skill helps you learn things faster over time. By stimulating neurons in the brain, more neural pathways are formed, and electrical impulses travel faster across them as you attempt to process new information. The more pathways that are formed, the faster impulses can travel. Learning rewires your brain!

OVER ONE HUNDRED SKILLS TO LEARN

Whether it's for business or personal reasons, there are learning opportunities all around you. Become a more productive person, increase your understanding of others, and fight boredom!

Crafts and Hobbies: (for example, learn to play guitar, piano, or harmonica)

Personal Finance and Business: (for example, learn create a personal budget or track receipts)

Health and Wellness: (for example, learn basic self-defense or how to master the mind-body connection)

Spirituality, Mindfulness, and Self-Improvement: (for example, learn to meditate or to improve your research skills)

______

______

______

______

______

______

House and Home: (for example, learn basic home repairs or how to organize and declutter your home)

______

______

______

______

______

______

Volunteer and Survival: (for example, learn dog walking or how to perform CPR)

The next few pages will help you think about various learning experiences that can round out your work-life balance and get you motivated. Some of these headings are for items you'll know right away; others are waiting for you to discover them.

My Favorite TEDx Topics

My Favorite Podcasts

My Favorite YouTube Channels

Books I Want to Read this Year

Documentaries I Want to Watch this Year

JOURNAL IT!

Where would you like to retire? What does retirement look like for you?

What's holding you back from accomplishing a goal? How can you overcome the challenge?

By the end of this chapter, you should have a good idea of how to prioritize your day and how to manage breaks, and a have made good start on what you can do in the space of a day to ensure you remain focused and on task when you are working. Most of your workday will consist of work tasks, but it's wise to remember to take the time out you need to recharge. We hope you'll investigate the tools and apps we suggested and find the ones that work for you. Next, we'll tackle scheduling and planning, which is key to your success as a remote worker.

coffee
123
456
789
YOUR
WORK
from
HOME
LIFE
YE
AH

CHAPTER 4

UNDERSTAND THE BASICS OF PLANNING AND SCHEDULING

Planning and setting goals[15] can help keep you focused and on course. Planning and scheduling when you work from home are both a little more complicated in many ways than in a traditional workplace, where you are in constant communication with the people you work closely with and can more easily be reminded of upcoming deadlines. Whether you're planning a personal goal or work-related goals, we find planning out the details saves time and frustration. This essential planner should serve as a guideline for setting goals for the day, the week, your whole life!

THE ESSENTIAL PLANNER

Step 1: Review your yearly goals.

Every Sunday, schedule a check-in with yourself to make sure you have everything in order for Monday and the rest of the week. Review any yearly goals you've set for yourself.

Make sure your goals are SMART goals—specific, measurable, attainable, realistic, and time-based. This makes it easier to define and achieve them.

Step 2: Keeping your goals in mind, review your monthly priorities and plans. Make note of any appointments or events that you need to plan around.

Step 3: Once you've determined this month's priorities, do a brain dump. Make a detailed list of every little thing you need and want to get done this week. This list should include tasks related to your monthly priorities, but also other necessary tasks like grocery shopping. Write down assignments, chores, time for yourself, and time for the important people in your life. Go through the list, and if it's too exhaustive, see if there's anything that could be moved to another week, if it's not urgent now. Figure out what absolutely needs to get done this week based on your monthly priorities. Set these tasks as your weekly priorities. Keep your weekly priorities list to three to seven items.

Step 4: Create a bulleted list of action steps for each priority on your to-do list. Think about action steps that will help you get your priorities completed, or even just started. These actions steps are also called "process goals." A process goal is what you actually need to achieve in order to achieve a larger goal. For example, if you want to increase sales by 25 percent, then your process goal would be to call five potential clients daily.

Step 5: Make your schedule, using an online calendar which can be accessed from multiple devices—schedule meetings/appointments, set up reminders, block time, and set up recurring events. On top of an online calendar, a calendar tool creates a daily routine, puts time limits on tasks, keeps your time under control, and helps you plan for breaks. For each day of the week, choose the one action step you will take. This will help you to stay focused and accomplish the most important thing first. Then add less important, but necessary, to-do tasks. Decide how much time to give to each item on your task list based on the time available and the urgency of each task. Allow for some buffer time. You need time to recharge and refocus.

Step 6: Benjamin Franklin said, "If you fail to plan, you are planning to fail!" Every night, at the same time, review your schedule for the next day.

Anticipate obstacles and have a contingency plan. Declutter your calendar when necessary.

Step 7: Refer back to your list often during the day. **Regroup every hour.** Sometimes, you might have to **bargain with yourself.** "If you don't want to do something, make a deal with yourself to do at least five minutes of it," says Instagram founder Kevin Systrom. "After five minutes, you'll end up doing the whole thing." Use visual reminders to keep you going. These could be inspiring quotes that you print and display around your home or office to keep you motivated.

Step 8: Regularly review the **past week**. David Allen championed this time-management habit and suggested the following steps: Get clear by emptying your inbox, wrapping up any loose ends, and tidying up; review your upcoming calendar, projects, actions lists, and checklists and ditching the inessentials; and get creative by finding unique ways to slip projects you've been putting off into your schedule.

Step 9: Only occasionally track your progress on goals. According to psychologist Kelly McGonigal, "although it runs counter to everything we believe about achieving our goals, focusing on progress can hold us back from success." Instead, McGonigal suggests that you "View your actions as evidence that you are committed to your goal" and remind yourself why you want to reach your goal.

THE ESSENTIAL PLANNER

Step 1: My Yearly Goals are:

They are

- Specific
- Measurable
- Attainable
- Realistic
- Time-based

Step 2: My Monthly Priorities are:

Step 3: Weekly Brain Dump

____

____

____

____

____

Steps 5-6: I have...

- ☐ made my schedule
- ☐ reviewed my schedule

Steps 7-9: I will...

- ☐ regroup every hour
- ☐ bargain with myself
- ☐ regularly review the past week
- ☐ only occasionally track my progress and goal

Step 4: My Weekly Priorities

1. ______________________________

Action Steps: ______________________________

____

____

2. ______________________________

Action Steps: ______________________________

____

____

3. ______________________________

Action Steps: ______________________________

____

____

THE WEEKLY TO-DO LIST

Monday	Tuesday	Wednesday	Important:
Thursday	Friday	Saturday	Sunday

Notes:

THE DAILY TO-DO LIST

- ☐
- ☐
- ☐
- ☐
- ☐
- ☐
- ☐
- ☐
- ☐
- ☐
- ☐
- ☐
- ☐
- ☐
- ☐
- ☐
- ☐

TEN MINUTES TO REFLECT ON YOUR DAY

Today I felt... ______________________________

____

Best Moment of the Day: ______________________________

3 Things That Went Well Today

3 Things That I Struggled With

What I learned from my challenges:

New ideas to explore:

JOURNAL IT!

What are your top five interests? How can you incorporate these interests into your daily activities?

What does "success" mean to you? How would you know that you've had a "successful life"?

Remember, all plans are just general guideposts to keep you on track. It's normal and perfectly acceptable to shift your goals as you learn and develop. You may not meet all your goals; that's also okay. This is why reevaluating your long-term goals periodically is so important. Some goals will be harder to reach than others, and even the best time managers find that they need to replan for contingencies that arise unexpectedly. Find a method that works best for you and stick with it, but build some flexibility and room for innovation into your scheduling. Chances are, you'll need it.

Now that you've mapped out a plan for goals and have an idea of what you want to accomplish, it's time to focus on how you can meet those goals when it feels like the distractions are endless.

CHAPTER 5

SET BOUNDARIES BETWEEN HOME AND WORK WHEN WORK IS AT HOME

When work is on the other side of a thin door, or even just across the kitchen, the distractions of a busy household—any household, even if you live alone—can keep you from reaching your peak efficiency. In this chapter, we offer ideas to help you find a perfect life-work balance,[16] ways to avoid distractions, explain how to avoid the temptation of social media, offer ways of dealing with people who steal time and energy, lay out a thirty-day plan to deep clean and declutter your home and office, discuss how to delegate household tasks to family members, help you plan meals, and suggest ways you can pat yourself on the back when you succeed at staying focused. It's a lot to cover, but by the end of the chapter, you should be ready to move forward with clarity and insight into what will work best for you in your new home office.

THE PERFECT WORK-LIFE BALANCE

1. **Understand what "balance" means for you.** Try to accept that there is no "perfect" work-life balance, and every person has individual needs. What works for someone else may not be right for you, and other people may not understand your needs at first.
2. **Set a schedule—and stick to it.** Limit your work hours. You have to plan in advance when you'll "leave" the office. It's a good idea to block out the last twenty minutes before you plan to sign off, to wrap up loose ends, so you aren't trying to send "one more email" after you were already supposed to turn off your computer.
3. **Make reasons to "leave work."** Join groups or sign up for online exercises classes that meet after work hours. Make "Zoom happy hour" plans with friends ahead of time so you can't back out and

just stick to your work. Schedule recurring social activities, like a monthly book club or weekly dinner with your best friends. By having regular activities like this written into your calendar, you'll be able to plan around them (instead of planning your social life around work).

4. **Take a break.** Be deliberate about taking time before work, after work, or on your lunch break to step away from your home office. Call your significant other, your mom, or your best friend, and ask what's going on with them, avoiding the temptation to discuss anything even remotely work-related.
5. **Make time for yourself and your loved ones by blocking out "me time" in your calendar.** Schedule vacation time or personal activities. It's important to remember that free time doesn't have to be available time—don't feel obligated to use it to get other things done, like errands or phone calls. Join an online yoga class or enjoy some light-hearted TV, spend an hour playing with the dog, or browse for random treasures on Amazon. Remember that scheduling downtime requires a combination of time management (deciding when to get the work done), working ahead when possible (so you have more time later), and keeping a to-do list.
6. **Know and set expectations.** When you take some time off, ask your boss if they expect you to check emails or listen to voice

messages while you're gone. While it's often necessary to stay at least a little connected, make sure you proactively set some boundaries. Feel free to let your boss know that you'll only be able to check your phone and email occasionally—say, once a day, or a few times a week. Most bosses will be fine if you only respond to critical messages until after you return home to the office.

7. **Set boundaries:** Avoid time vampires. Limit time-wasting activities and people (more on this later).
8. **Don't be afraid to unplug.** Turn off technology. Carve out some time on the weekends—at least a few hours, but ideally a whole day—to stay away from screens. Put your computer and phone away and turn off the TV, then do something physical or creative that you really love. Go for a run. Draw. Write. Your mind will be a little more refreshed and a little sharper by the end of it.
9. **Prioritize your health.** Schedule time to exercise and meditate. Schedule regular checkups with your primary care physician and dentist. Make sure you are eating a well-balanced, nutritious diet. It's easy to lose yourself in a bag of chips when you're alone in your home office. Reach for fruits or nuts instead.
10. **Delegate tasks—at work and at home.** Don't be afraid to outsource or delegate tasks to people you work with remotely, if you can. Figure out which tasks are crucially yours to complete,

and which ones you can hand off to someone else. Ask for help and delegate properly. Get creative with what chores you can outsource and automate. You may find that hiring out some of the more menial tasks you need to accomplish (especially if you own your own business) will free you up for more creative endeavors. Whether you find a nearby grocery delivery service or have a professional tinker with your PowerPoint presentation, free up some time in your schedule to do something else.

11. **Set goals and priorities (and stick to them)**
12. **Let go of perfectionism.** Goals aren't mandates, and you'll need to learn to be flexible with your priorities, because they have a tendency to shift when new priorities present themselves.
13. **Practice self-care.** Consider some highlights of your perfect day. What would you really enjoy doing? What's absolutely necessary for you to get done? Identify what tools or extras would make the mandatory work easier to complete. Enjoying aromatherapy while you grade papers? Going on a run? Figure out what can help you and build it into your day.
14. **Do your least favorite chore at the beginning of each week.** Without this burden, the week will feel entirely more manageable. Also, instead of saving all of your life chores for Sunday, get them out of the way as soon as possible, either by doing them first thing Saturday morning or dispersing them

throughout the week. That way, instead of spending your last few hours of free time on Sunday night scrubbing the bathtub, you'll be able to fill it with something fun and relaxing.

15. **Use your time wisely.** Stop multitasking. Instead, track and limit how much time you're spending on tasks. Keep a time diary. Then eliminate distractions and set self-imposed deadlines. Learn to speed-read. Learn to skip when you read. Learn keyboard shortcuts. Improve your typing speed to save time. Shorten your emails. Take shorter showers and lighten your cleaning standards. Shop online. Speed up your internet with a broadband connection. Keep up the speed of your computer. Automate what you can: autopay your bills; use direct deposit; plan your meals in advance and cook them in bulk. (Think "half-time." For example, if you're cooking dinner, make the twice the normal amount and freeze half of it. This way you're not spending that time again preparing your meal on another night.) Make use of waiting time. Measure twice, cut once: double-check your work so that you don't spend time going back and correcting your mistakes.

CHECKLIST—THE PERFECT WORK LIFE BALANCE

- ☐ Understand what "balance" means for you.
- ☐ Set a schedule—and stick to it.
- ☐ Make reasons to "leave work."
- ☐ Take a break.
- ☐ Make time for yourself and your loved ones by blocking out "me time" in your calendar.
- ☐ Know and set expectations.
- ☐ Set boundaries.
- ☐ Don't be afraid to unplug.
- ☐ Prioritize your health.
- ☐ Delegate tasks—at work and at home.
- ☐ Set goals and priorities (and stick to them).
- ☐ Let go of perfectionism.
- ☐ Practice self-care.
- ☐ Do your least favorite chore at the beginning of each week.
- ☐ Use your time wisely.

AVOID DISTRACTIONS

In order to reach a good work-life balance, you need to understand what work items need to get done for the day, and get them done on time, so you aren't scrambling after hours to finish up. That can feel impossible if the outside world is trying to barge into your office space. Here are some tips we've found are effective at avoiding distractions[17] so that you can get through your to-do-for-work lists.

TIME MANAGEMENT: FIFTEEN WAYS TO AVOID DISTRACTIONS

1. **Take stock:** Before you get started, pick a day in your week to keep track of everything you do. Identify the distractions that come your way, and which take the most of your time. This exercise will help you pinpoint and distinguish the legitimate distractions from those that could be delegated to others or

put aside for later. Reflect on your productivity constantly. Work on your professional development by listening to podcasts and reading bestselling books like David Allen's *Getting Things Done*. Go on an information diet. Find a mentor. A mentor will share with you the tips and tricks that have worked for them, as well as the mistakes to avoid. Monitor your progress against your goals. Track your habits to better understand yourself.

2. **Pinpoint the cause of internal distraction.** First, check up on yourself: distractions can be internal as well as external, so start by looking within. If you're all over the place, ask yourself what's really going on. What's the source of your flightiness or anxiety? What do you need to be working on in your life? Control your internal distractions. Keep your vision and goals in mind and have a calming mantra. Visualize yourself working.
3. **Remove external distractions.** Once you have your internal priorities sorted out, look at more external causes. Is it your office setup? An intrusive coworker? A lack of skill, ideas, or time for something you need to be doing? Burnout? When you can identify the cause, you can fix the effect. If the squeaky ceiling fan is driving you nuts, get it fixed. If you have an upstairs neighbor who practices tap dance while you're trying to work, get yourself a good white-noise machine or work around their practice sessions. Whatever is keeping you from focusing,

eliminate it from your environment, and if you can't eliminate it completely, find a way to work around it.

4. **Communicate expectations with anyone who will be home with you.** Set ground rules so that children, roommates, siblings, parents, and spouses respect your space during work hours. Just because you're working from home doesn't mean you're home and available. Setting expectations brings better family balance because everyone knows what to expect. Make your intentions known. Tell the people around you, "I need to focus for the next ninety minutes. Please do not interrupt me." And feel free to redirect them if they do interrupt. With children in the home, this can be especially difficult. Plan a reward for small kids when it's time for you to break at the end of your designated work block. Or ask whomever is minding the kids to take them for a walk so you can work uninterrupted. Close the door. Shutting yourself off from the rest of your home not only sends a signal to those around you that you are at work, it also tells you it's time to focus on the task at hand and get to work.

5. **Turn off the background noise.** Wear noise-canceling headphones if necessary. Try a natural soundscape like a rainforest or trickling stream as a soundtrack that can both soothe you and quiet your mind so you can refocus. Or move to another location in the house, if you find your office space is in a high-traffic area of your home or a place that is prone to noise

and activity. Keep in mind that some teleworkers have reported that keeping something like the History Channel running in the background, at a low volume, helps them get more work done. In this case, keep the TV or the radio on in the background.

6. **Break down the items on your to-do list.** Especially when distractions are many, make tasks smaller and break down your large projects into smaller tasks to help you concentrate and give you a sense of accomplishment and progress. Take it one thing at a time and reduce the chaos of your day by focusing on two to three important tasks. Focus on only the smallest details of your work one by one.
7. **Schedule your work in batches;** for example, spend one day solely dedicated to writing, another to meetings. Or implement a "No-Meetings Wednesdays" rule (like Facebook and Asana did); as opposed to wasting your time in a meeting, you can focus on important individual tasks.
8. **Set a deadline and stick to it.** Shrink your mental deadlines. If you believe it's going to take you an hour to do something, give yourself forty minutes instead. By shrinking your mental deadline you'll work faster, as well as improve your focus.
9. **Plan for interruptions** because, try all you might, there will occasionally be interruptions. Plan for these in advance by

having some flexibility in your schedule so that you don't get logjammed.

10. **Schedule your distractions.** Turn your distractions into rewards that you can focus on, briefly, during your scheduled breaks. Limiting distractions to break times will keep them from taking over your day and give you something to look forward to.
11. **Go offline.** Use the internet sparingly. Close your browser, and say no to checking your email. Tune it out. Stay away from social media. To avoid "accidentally" finding yourself on Facebook, remove social media networks from your browser shortcuts and log out of every account. Turn off the TV. Use a TiVo, a DVR, or a streaming service.
12. **Put down the phone or switch it off.** You can always pick it up and check for messages during a break. Use the phone as one of those distraction rewards you only reach for during breaks. And remember, not every message needs to be returned immediately. Most of them can wait until the end of day. **If your job requires that you keep your phone on, screen your calls.** People who don't work from home have a hard time understanding that while you are home, you are actually working. Do not pick up your personal phone during work hours, and they'll get the hint. Set up a separate phone number that you only use for calls with colleagues and clients. It doesn't have

to be a landline, a second cell phone, or even a SIM card. It can be a free VoIP service, such as Google Voice or a Skype number.

13. **Avoid housework during work hours.** Instead, schedule specific time for household activities—break times or after hours. While it makes sense to do some housework when you work at home, it can be one of the biggest distractions. Establish "maintenance days." Group your cleaning, laundry, and errands on specific days. This way they're not hanging over your head when working on more pressing matters. Prepare your meals the night before, so that you can actually use your mealtimes to eat instead of performing nonwork tasks that spend energy better used at your desk.
14. **Take sick days.** Keep in mind that sometimes it's best to rest and get better so that you can be your most productive self in the long term.
15. **Use focus tools.** Focus@Will is an app that not only removes distractions, it also increases productivity. How? It discovers the type of music that puts your brain into a "flow state."

CHECKLIST—15 WAYS TO AVOID DISTRACTIONS

- ☐ Take stock.
- ☐ Pinpoint the cause of internal distraction.
- ☐ Remove external distractions.
- ☐ Communicate expectations with anyone who will be home with you.
- ☐ Turn off the background noise.
- ☐ Break down the items on your to-do list.
- ☐ Schedule your work in batches.
- ☐ Set a deadline and stick to it.
- ☐ Plan for interruptions.
- ☐ Schedule your distractions.
- ☐ Go offline.
- ☐ Put down the phone or switch it off. Or screen your calls.
- ☐ Avoid housework during work hours.
- ☐ Take sick days.
- ☐ Use focus tools.

In an increasingly digital age, there is a tendency to lose oneself online. If you find yourself getting dragged into a "time suck" on social media, closely examine what you are doing with that time. Remember people post only part of their lives online, and usually what we see is an idealized, sanitized version of reality. No one is picture-perfect.

Ask yourself these questions: Do you check your Instagram or Facebook (or any other social media platform) excessively? Do you find yourself obsessing over how many "likes" you get and become agitated when you don't get enough? Do you equate the number of followers or friends on social media to popularity or likability? Do you feel envious or jealous when you see your friends' "picture-perfect" lives on social media? Do you feel like you're always missing out or being left out of significant events?

If you answer yes to most of these questions, it might be time to disconnect!

SIX WAYS TO AVOID THE SOCIAL MEDIA TEMPTATION[18]

1. **Keep yourself busy and keep track of your time for a week.** At the end of the week, do a tally of the time you spent on social media. How much of that time was just scrolling your newsfeeds? Chances are, it's a lot more than you realized. You can also use apps like Stay Focused to limit your social media access on your phone.
2. **Remove social networks from your browser shortcuts.** If it's harder to get to, you're less likely to open up social media sites in your browser. Log out of every account, and work primarily in a private or "incognito" browser window to ensure that you stay signed out of all your accounts. Don't enable auto-login. If you have to put in your password each time, it'll keep it from being a knee-jerk reaction. Bonus points for adding two-factor authentication: more security, and another hurdle to hopping on social networks. You can also choose to temporarily block social media sites from your computer using a tool like SelfControl (Mac) or Cold Turkey (Windows). The lack of easy access will keep you from browsing Twitter in the corner of the kitchen while your

family is spending quality time without you or when you should be getting work completed.

3. **Power down before bed**, and don't sleep with your phone next to your bed. Charge your phone in a room you don't enter often. Not having your smartphone next to your bed when you wake up will work wonders for your check-your-email-first-thing-in-the-morning habit. You'll need to get your hands on an actual alarm clock so that your morning routine doesn't include using your phone as an alarm. Have Alexa wake you up instead or purchase a clock radio and set it to wake you up with some tunes that will invigorate you.
4. **Leave your phone in a drawer** (out of sight, out of mind), or leave it in another room. Alternatively, keep your phone on silent so you don't get pinged every few minutes. Remove notifications from your phone. (That's right, no pop-ups to tell you that so-and-so wants to play Candy Crush, nothing to taunt you to open an app.) Or turn your phone off completely during your work cycle. You can always turn it back on when you take a break. Some people choose to put their phone on airplane mode and disconnect Wi-Fi. It's easier mentally than having your phone turned off, but, really, it's not connected to anything.
5. **Don't live by the "pics or it didn't happen" motto/mentality.** Not every meal you eat needs to be posted to social media. Find a

hobby outside of the internet world. Plan activities that don't mix well with phones or computers, like going for a walk or a bike ride. Go on a walk or run without your phone. Practice learning to disconnect during your free time, and it will be easier to disconnect when you should be working.

6. **Use Inbox Pause** and only unpause it when you actually want to check email. If something is urgent, people will find a way to get in touch with you. This will reduce your urge to keep checking your email, since nothing new will be there until you take the step of unpausing.

HOW TO DEAL WITH TIME (AND ENERGY) VAMPIRES

Energy vampires are people who feed on your compassion and willingness to listen to the never-ending drama of their lives. While energy vampires can steal your positive energy, they can't succeed unless you allow them to affect you.[19]

1. **Reduce contact.** As much as possible, back away from the energy vampires in your life. Place your focus on what you need to

accomplish rather than being a willing ear.

2. **Remember to plan all phone and video calls.** Protect yourself from unnecessary phone time with caller ID; ignore unimportant emails, and just say no: ditch commitments that waste your time, energy, and attention. Use a system that will automatically end the call after five, fifteen, or thirty minutes, and warn your interlocutor that there is a time limit.
3. **Cut them out of your life (if you can).** You can do this by either backing away slowly, or by being direct. Don't agree to coffee dates. Don't answer the phone. Don't feel the need to return calls.
4. **Listen when they vent, but don't talk** (and know the difference between "venting" and "dumping"). Don't offer any emotional advice. Don't engage them further by asking questions about the situation. Keep smiling.
5. **Set boundaries.** Use "I" statements. Feel free to express your own needs. "I need to go now." "I'm sorry you are having such a hard time. I need to get (this task) finished." "I'm sorry I can't help you with that." Be specific. "That sounds frustrating, but I'd prefer that we only talk about work right now."
6. **Change the focus of the conversation:** Don't be afraid to interject and redirect the conversation. "Can we talk about ____?"

7. **Say no.** *The Power of No: Because One Little Word Can Bring Health, Abundance, and Happiness*, by James Altucher and Claudia Azula Altucher, is an excellent book to help you learn how to say no more effectively.
8. **Leave if you need to.** Or get off the phone. Say, "I see. Let me know when you're ready to talk about (work-related matter). I need to go right now."

CHECKLIST—DEALING WITH TIME VAMPIRES

- ☐ Reduce contact.
- ☐ Remember to plan all phone and video calls.
- ☐ Cut them out of your life (if you can).
- ☐ Listen when they vent, but don't talk.
- ☐ Set boundaries.
- ☐ Change the focus of the conversation.
- ☐ Say no.
- ☐ Leave if you need to.

Aja Frost suggests twenty-one ways to leave a never-ending conversation without being rude. Here are some examples:

- "I've got another call in a couple minutes; thanks so much for speaking with me, and I'll talk to you again [soon/in X days]."
- "It sounds like we've covered everything we needed to, so I'll let you go. Thank you for such a productive meeting!"
- "Looks like we've hit everything on the agenda. If no one has anything else to discuss, see you all at next week's meeting."
- "I really appreciate you taking the time to speak with me. Have a fantastic rest of your day, and I'll look for your [email/notes/report/follow-up]."
- "Wow, I can't believe it's already [time]. Do you mind if I hang up and finish up my to-do list?"

DELEGATE

When you work from home, it can be too easy to lapse into taking on all of the responsibilities for home upkeep and meal planning and preparation. Unless you live alone, everyone who lives with you should and can take part in running the household, and your life will be much easier if you delegate tasks to your family members or roommates. Have a family meeting and assign chores to everyone. Be willing to teach the kids some new skills if need be. Learn to let go of perfect results, but be willing to show them a correct method or step in if they slack or make mistakes. Remember to be patient. It takes time to form new habits, and it takes time to learn independent living skills.

A good way to start a new routine is to do a thirty-day deep clean and declutter. Once your home is in order, it'll be easier to see what's out of place and clean up regularly.

THIRTY-DAY DEEP CLEAN AND DECLUTTER

Day	Cleaning Task	Who	Done!
1	Fridge		
2	Stove and oven		
3	Kitchen cupboards and drawers		
4	Pantry		
5	Microwave and kitchen sink		
6	Dining tables and chairs		
7	Laundry room		
8	Linen closet		
9	Baseboards		
10	Living room		
11	Entertainment area		
12	Coat closet		

Day	Cleaning Task	Who	Done!
13	Blinds and curtains		
14	Second bathroom		
15	Medicine cabinet		
16	Master bed and drawers		
17	Master closet		
18	Office area		
19	Books and games		
20	Garage and storage bins		
21	Kids' beds and drawers		
22	Kids' closet		
23	Toys		
24	Wash walls		
25	Vents and smoke detectors		
26	Stairs and railings		
27	Windows inside		
28	Windows outside		
29	Basement		
30	Attic		

AGE-APPROPRIATE CHORES FOR KIDS

Even the youngest members of your family should and can have a role in making sure the household is running smoothly. If you start children learning at a young age, they not only learn how to do the task you're teaching them, they also learn the satisfaction of doing a job well. Just remember to be consistent, assertive, and, most of all, patient. Here are some age-appropriate chores for the kids.

AGES TWO TO THREE (TODDLER)

- ☐ Put toys and books away
- ☐ Put dirty clothes in the hamper; take folded laundry to the bedroom
- ☐ Sort shoes and put away unused footwear
- ☐ Wipe lower parts of windows with a cloth
- ☐ Put dishes in the sink after a meal
- ☐ Clean up crumbs with a hand vacuum

- ☐ Feed pet (with assistance)
- ☐ Pick up sticks, toys, and other items in yard
- ☐ Clean all outdoor toys with rag and soapy water

AGES FOUR TO FIVE (PRESCHOOL)

- ☐ Make bed
- ☐ Match socks and put away clothes
- ☐ Tidy room; dust with feather duster
- ☐ Clean windows with cloth after an adult sprays them
- ☐ Feed and hydrate pets and water indoor plants
- ☐ Wipe up spills and help fill dishwasher
- ☐ Empty household waste baskets into trash to go out
- ☐ Get the mail

AGES SIX TO NINE (ELEMENTARY)

- ☐ Help fold laundry
- ☐ Sort their clothes and remove ones that are too tight/small, help pack outgrown clothes for donation
- ☐ Spray and clean window with cloth or newspaper, wipe counters and

tables, and empty dishwasher (no sharp objects)

- ☐ Sweep floors
- ☐ Help with food shopping; put away groceries; set the table; clear dishes after meals; pack lunches and make own snacks
- ☐ Help put mulch into flower beds; pull weeds; help rake leaves; clean outdoor furniture; and sweep porch/patio/deck/walkway
- ☐ Sort outdoor toys and remove ones that are broken or outgrown
- ☐ Prep outdoor equipment (example, put air in bike tires, basketballs, etc.)
- ☐ Collect garbage on garbage night

AGES TEN TO TWELVE (PRETEEN)

- ☐ Take out trash
- ☐ Wash, dry, and fold laundry; clean and organize closet and dresser; make a list of donation items as they are sorted/packed
- ☐ Mop and vacuum
- ☐ Plan a weekly menu; help prep for meals; make simple meals (easy breakfast and lunch); wash pots and pans
- ☐ Clean toilets
- ☐ Clean windows

- ☐ Clean out vehicle
- ☐ Take garbage out, take cans to curb and bring back

AGES THIRTEEN TO SIXTEEN (TEENS)

- ☐ Babysit siblings; oversee the younger children's chores (or at least inspect them)
- ☐ Help with grocery shopping and errands
- ☐ Plan and prepare meals; clean out refrigerator/freezer; load the dishwasher
- ☐ Clean tub/shower
- ☐ Make minor repairs and keep up sports equipment (e.g. adjust bike seat, clean and oil wheels on skateboards)
- ☐ Mow lawn
- ☐ Help turn over garden, water new grass, and prep flower beds

AGES SEVENTEEN TO EIGHTEEN (YOUNG ADULTS)

- ☐ Do their own laundry; iron clothes
- ☐ Keep up their room and their personal space

- ☐ Cook whole meals and clean up
- ☐ Help remove screens for deep cleaning and clean and dust windowsills
- ☐ Help with simple home repairs
- ☐ Basic car maintenance (oil change or check the tires)
- ☐ Wash vehicles
- ☐ Yard work
- ☐ Organize a budget for themselves
- ☐ Keep up with their chores, work schedules, homework, and sports activities

THE MEAL PLANNER

Meal planning ahead of time is another way to make sure the household is running smoothly. It'll help you with shopping lists and cut down on preparation time if you use the following worksheet to plan out your meals in advance:

Monday

Tuesday

Wednesday

Snacks

Thursday

Friday

Grocery Shopping List:

Saturday

Sunday

BE FLEXIBLE

When you work from home, you need to learn to expect the unexpected, and adapt to suit the needs of your job—and your life! Things happen. So, don't beat yourself up if your day isn't as productive as you might have liked it to be. One of the beauties of having a flexible schedule is that you can—and must—be adaptable. Sometimes, for instance, you need to extend your day or start early to accommodate someone else's time zone. When you do, be sure to wrap up earlier than usual or sleep in a bit the next morning to make up for it.

Don't be too hard on yourself. It takes serious focus to do any full-time office job from an unconventional space. Sometimes, you will let your attention drift. If you find yourself working one minute and daydreaming the next, don't reprimand yourself too harshly. Cut yourself some slack, and then go back to work.

Pat yourself on the back.[20] Take time to congratulate yourself for a job well-done. Make yourself a fresh pot of coffee or to take a long break after finishing a burdensome task. Rewarding yourself appropriately throughout the day gives you positive feedback for your accomplishments and keeps things from getting stale.

WAYS TO PAT YOURSELF ON THE BACK

REWARD YOURSELF FOR TEN DOLLARS OR LESS

1. **Stay-at-Home Movie Night:** Pop some popcorn, make some snacks, and kick your feet up with that movie you've been wanting to watch. You can stream most movies shortly after their cinema release on a streaming service or rent them for much less than the cost of a theater movie experience, and the best part is, you don't have to leave home to do it.
2. **Fancy Coffee:** Go ahead and splurge on that fancy cup of Ethiopian coffee from the fancy coffee shop downtown. If you don't have coffee out all that often, it is a special treat that's relatively affordable. Or pick up a pound of your favorite brew at the local roasters to enjoy at home as a reward for meeting your goals.

3. **Buy Yourself Something Nice (and Cheap),** like a new journal or the electronic version of that book you've been dying to read. Be creative when you're hunting down that little something extra to enjoy.
4. **Go Camping—In Your Backyard:** If you have the yard space, pitch a tent in the backyard, roast some marshmallows on the fire (or your barbecue grill, if your local fire ordinances don't allow backyard campfires), and tell some ghost stories. You don't have to travel far to see the stars, and a night out in the backyard can feel like a trip to a national park with the right friends (or family) to keep you company.
5. **Subscribe.** We were surprised by how many magazine subscriptions cost ten dollars or less! This is the gift (to yourself) that keeps giving (twelve times, anyway). And each month when your magazine comes in, you'll have a happy reminder to keep rocking those money goals.

MAKE YOUR OWN LIST: OTHER WAYS TO PAT YOURSELF ON THE BACK

Like everything else, avoiding distractions takes time, practice, and patience. It may be difficult at first, but if you are consistent, in no time you'll turn these ideas into habits, and the things distracting you today will only be minor in a few weeks. If you follow the tips in this chapter, your household will support your efforts to get your work done with fewer interruptions.

CHAPTER 6

STAY CONNECTED

When you work from home, it can feel like the world is going on all around you and you are in a separate reality, off to the side and forgotten. It's up to you to make connections with the people you work with and communicate your needs and contributions. This isn't so much about gaining attention as it is about making sure that you are part of a well-working system. Sometimes it can feel like you're overcompensating for your absence. It's important to strike the right balance between pestering your coworkers and allowing yourself to fall to the wayside. It's important that the people you work with see that you are making a positive contribution to the team and can be relied on to work independently. The best way to do this is to stay connected.

Schedule time to check in. Working from home might make you feel cut off from the larger operation happening in the office. Use instant messaging and videoconferencing tools to check in with coworkers and to remind you how your work is contributing to the big picture. It's a good idea to set up specific times when your coworkers know you will be available to answer questions and collaborate.

Be proactive. If you're working for a company with a strong remote culture, you may need to be more proactive about nurturing relationships. It's a good idea to attend nonmandatory meetings and get some individual face time with colleagues. If your company holds an annual picnic or holiday office party, make it a point to go, even if you aren't all that comfortable in social situations. Drop into the office for meetings every once in a while, or schedule a day at a regular interval (once a week, once every two weeks, or monthly) to work on-site. It makes a big difference if people can place a face with your name.

Be creative. Schedule virtual happy hours with your closest coworkers. Or send thank-you or birthday cards. Have some flowers or a treat (like donuts) delivered if someone goes out of their way for you. Take time to learn about the culture in the office and be a part of it when you can. Sometimes this means stretching to reach out across what feels like a gigantic digital divide. Trust that there are humans on the other side.

Overcommunicate. Tell everyone who needs to know about your schedule and availability often. Start a shared calendar and populate it with your deadlines and hours so people know when you're working and what you're working on. When you finish a project or important task, say so. Mark it on the calendar. Repeat yourself. Joke about how you must have mentioned your upcoming vacation six times already, then mention it again. Follow up in writing when you can, so there is a written reminder of whatever it is you need to communicate clearly. Remember, when you are home, the office may be busy with people coming in and out, and it's easy to get lost in the shuffle.

Be positive. When you work remotely, others don't always know how to interpret your tone in writing. Make it a point to be overly positive when communicating. Embrace the exclamation point. Find your favorite emojis—especially if you are using humor to make a point. But avoid sarcasm, because it can come across as anger or passive-aggression. Strive for clear, concise communication.

ONLINE MEETING ETIQUETTE: TEN THINGS TO REMEMBER[21]

No one needs a visual reminder that, most of the time, you have the freedom to work in your pajamas and not fix your hair. If you have a scheduled video conference or meeting, take some time to prep for it. Here are some tips:

1. Dress the part. Touch up your appearance. Brush your hair and teeth. Put on some business attire and look like a professional.
2. Test your audio, mic, and video ahead of time to make sure they are working. No one wants to wait for you to deal with technological issues, and it'll help the meeting go faster if you are ready and functioning ahead of time.
3. Connect from a quiet, carpeted room, with a neutral background and good lighting. Create a professional remote office that looks pleasant to the eye and is not distracting to those on the other end.
4. Use your laptop, and not your phone. Raise your webcam to eye level and use a good microphone. When you're not talking, mute your mic. Remember that headphones and a microphone make calls sound much clearer for everyone.
5. Turn off notifications and avoid multitasking.
6. Look at the camera, not the screen, when talking. Articulate as clearly as you can, and smile.
7. Always create an agenda. Without an agenda, meetings can go awry fast.

8. Stay on time as much as possible. When you have two-hour-long meetings, it can be easy to dread them!
9. Toward the end of the meeting, do some time checks. Start at fifteen minutes before the end of the meeting to stay on track, and then five minutes. Define next steps. "We have fifteen minutes left. Let's plan ______." "In our last five minutes, let's plan _____."
10. Ask everyone for their input. Just like in a real meeting, sometimes people can hang back and not add their perspective, so do a "round robin" to ask everyone to contribute to the conversation!!

PROACTIVE, CREATIVE, POSITIVE: TEN HELPFUL RULES FOR REMOTE WORK COMMUNICATION

According to Becca from halfhalftravel.com,[22] if you've ever heard of "being seen and not heard," it's the opposite for someone working from home. "You want to be heard, and hopefully 'seen' (on video)!" she writes.

WHEN TO COMMUNICATE

1. When you have any doubt.
2. When you have questions.
3. At the slightest concern.
4. When you have or need feedback.
5. When you have results or success.
6. To share your schedule.
7. To give updates.

HOW TO COMMUNICATE

1. Frequently.
2. Eloquently.
3. Clearly.

FUN WAYS TO KEEP IN TOUCH WITH COWORKERS WHILE WORKING REMOTELY[23]

- Learn to embrace the joy of making a phone call.
- Try using video to connect with your coworkers, but remember to stay professional.
- See your weekly team meeting as something you can look forward to; it helps break the isolation of working from home alone.
- Try conferencing to collaborate on projects in real time.
- Speak up and bring something new to Slack channels.
- Make sure to update your Google Calendar, or your organization's calendar system.
- Use Trello for help managing projects, deadlines, and ideas.
- Start a "nonwork" channel in Slack or Teams.
- Schedule virtual dinner and lunch meetings.
- Pay attention to your coworkers' professional and personal successes.

- Start a book club for your company.
- Host a cooking competition for your coworkers.
- Create a nonwork-related email group for jokes and videos.
- Bring something positive into the start of each meeting, even if it's just a smile.
- Plan a talent show for your company and clients.
- Play online games with coworkers during off hours.
- Remind your coworkers that you are always available.
- Start a monthly lunch-and-learn.
- Start a program to pair mentors with newbies in your organization.
- Use WhatsApp to remain in contact with your coworkers.
- Connect with clients and vendors on social media.
- Use Q&A in Zoom or GoToWebinar for online interactions.
- Make a game of being the first to respond in group emails, and let people know you're available when they need you to be.
- Try joining a professional or alumni network to make more connections.
- FaceTime with someone every day.
- Surprise people with a voice call.

- Learn a new language by practicing online with a friend in another country.

STAY CONNECTED—TO OTHERS, TO YOUR PETS, AND TO NATURE

"No one can live without relationships. You may withdraw into the mountains, become a monk, a sannyasi, wander off into the desert by yourself, but you are related. You cannot escape from that absolute fact. You cannot exist in isolation."
—**Jiddu Krishnamurti**, Indian philosopher, speaker and writer

Humans are social animals. We crave feeling supported, valued, and connected. Even in the isolation of remote work, try to stay connected. Call your mother or your best friend. Revive old memories on a call or on FaceTime with an old friend. Order monogrammed stationery and send handwritten letters to family and friends (postcards will do, too). Write short text messages to your loved ones to tell them how special they are. Make paper dolls, then put them in envelopes and send them to your best friends.

Host an online book club or writing group. Get yourself some pen pals. If you play video games, connect with opponents via online communities such as Xbox Live, PlayStation Network, and Steam.

Spend some quality time with your family at home and ditch social media. Reminisce about old times and take out your old photo albums. Play board games, learn and play a new card game, or create your own bingo cards and have a tournament. Let your kids write and direct a stop-motion movie. Play twenty questions. Make a mancala counting game with an egg carton (Google the directions). Make shadow puppets. Cut out drawings of Where's Waldo and stick them in secret corners of your house.

Remember that the companionship that a pet offers is also a great way to reduce anxiety and stress. Play with your pet and teach them a new trick. Take photographs of them wearing costumes and/or hats and start an Instagram profile for your pet. Watch funny cat videos (always works). Make a homemade treat for your dog. Take your pet for a walk in nature.

In fact, interacting with nature is recognized as one way to improve mental health, so, while you're outside, enjoy every minute of fresh air. You can also bring nature into your home: plant a fragrant herb garden on your windowsill, repot your houseplants, plant a family garden, plant some flowers and let them decorate your room with a lovely scent, sing to your plants, create a nature scavenger hunt in your backyard, or build a treehouse. No backyard? No problem. Bring the outdoors indoors!

GOOGLE HOW TO...

- Play a game of find the treats ______
- Play the shell game ______
- Teach your dog to clean up his toys ______
- Use a stuffed Kong to keep your dog entertained ______
- Play a game of tug-of-war ______
- Teach your dog to help with chores ______
- Play interactive games ______
- Make your dog work for his food ______
- Teach your dog the names of their toys ______
- Teach your dog to "go find" their toys ______
- Work on some clicker training ______
- Play the which-hand game ______

- Play a game of hide-and-seek
- Get some puzzle toys for your dog
- Master the basics of obedience training
- Play a game of fetch
- Master the art of doggie massage
- Try some free shaping games
- Give your dog regular grooming sessions
- Play a game of tag
- Create your own indoor doggie obstacle course
- Teach your dog to chase bubbles
- Buy a new dog toy, make one, or rotate them
- Brush up on some old tricks
- Teach your dog the "go to" command
- Teach your dog to grab his leash
- Teach your dog to turn on/off lights
- Work on impulse control for better manners

- Make some simple dog treats ______________
- Teach them to say please by sitting ______________
- Snuggle up and relax on the couch ______________

ACTIVITIES AND IDEAS TO STAY CONNECTED

Isn't it strange to think that, in a world that's known for its twenty-four seven connectivity, we might actually need to try a little harder to stay connected to family and friends when working remotely? Yes, we have phones that give us instant access to the people we know. But there's something about creative ways of communicating[24] that seem like they get the job done just a little bit better.

Here are some ideas to stay connected:

1. Have a long-distance movie night.
2. Send virtual flowers.
3. Share friendship bracelets.

4. Send an e-card via Someecards.com, JibJab, or Blue Mountain.
5. Send some cool picture collages created on BeFunky Collage Maker.
6. Share a journal on Xanga.com or LiveJournal.com.
7. Video chat on Skype, Zoom, or WhatsApp!
8. Create a blog together on WordPress.com.
9. Sing karaoke together on SingSnap.com.
10. Read a book together.
11. Take an online compatibility test on SimilarMinds.com.
12. Play a game together or join a virtual world like Second Life, Kaneva, IMVU, and There.
13. Listen to music together on Live365.com or RadioTower.com.
14. Share an online calendar with Google Calendar.
15. Go on a virtual vacation together with 360Cities.net or EarthAlbum.com. You can also make your own radio station together on Blip.fm.
16. Surf the web together with StumbleUpon.
17. Play phone games such as Twenty Questions or Name That Tune.
18. Cook and eat together via Skype or Zoom.
19. Send a virtual hug with OnlineHugs.com.

20. Create a personal crossword puzzle with Crossword Puzzle Maker.
21. Find out what the stars have to say about your relationship on Astrology.com.
22. Send them a text for free via WhatsApp.
23. Make a card on the Hallmark website.
24. Watch a concert together on iConcerts.com.
25. Send video messages with Marco Polo.
26. Write a poem together with RhymeZone.com.
27. Send a personal cryptoquip on Quipquip.com.
28. Take a free class together, using the Guide to Online Schools to find some options.
29. Make a list together on Scribbless.com.
30. Quiz each other on MakeAQuiz.net.
31. Record a story via Audacity.
32. Send a GeoGreeting.
33. Make a Countdown.
34. Here are some "Mad Lib" sites you can use: Wacky Web Tales, Crazy Tales, and WordBlanks.com.
35. Set goals for each other.

36. Create a song on Clash.me or SongLyricsGenerator.com.
37. Make a song on JamStudio.com or with GarageBand.
38. Wordle lets you make your own word clouds.
39. Play charades. This popular party game can also be a very fun game to play with a friend on webcam.
40. Make a word search on ArmoredPenguin.com.
41. Watch YouTube and Vimeo together using Sync-video.com.
42. Exercise together. Set up a time when you both commit to exercise in your respective homes.
43. Share a virtual bulletin board on PinUp.com.
44. Figure out your Myers-Briggs Type on PersonalityPage.com.
45. Read My Lips. During a video chat, one of you will mute themself and the other has to read their lips to figure out what they are saying.

JOURNAL IT!

Is there someone from high school or college that you want to get in touch with again? How can you reach out to them?

CHAPTER 7

PRACTICE SELF-CARE

Love yourself first, and everything else falls in line. You really have to love yourself to get anything done in this world."

—Lucille Ball

Those of us who pay attention to their own physical and emotional health are better able to adapt to changes, build strong relationships, and recover from setbacks. Self-care is important. Improving your relationship with yourself makes you more resilient.

TWENTY TIPS FOR PERSONALIZING YOUR SELF-CARE STRATEGY

In the scramble to stay connected with coworkers and family and friends, it's easy to lose connection with yourself. Make sure you are taking some time out to pamper yourself. What that looks like is, again, an individual preference. If you're not in the habit of spoiling yourself rotten, start now, and remember to be mindful of your own needs for connection to yourself. Pay attention to your body and your mental health. Here are some suggestions for personalizing your self-care strategy.

1. DIY something beautiful. Snuggle on the couch—or put on all your sequins—and read your favorite books.
2. Try adult coloring books.
3. Daydream.
4. Pamper yourself with the bubbliest aromatic bath you can create, light some candles, and call one of your best friends for a long-overdue chat.
5. Put on your bathrobe, set up an in-home nail salon, and try some elaborate nail art techniques.

6. Learn new makeup and beauty techniques on YouTube.
7. Take some time to take care of your hair, nails, and skin using some homemade recipes.
8. Tweeze and glitter your eyebrows.
9. If you want to go for something a bit crazy, try dyeing/trimming your hair at home and transform your look. Or tease your hair really, really big.
10. Moisturize your entire body.
11. Make faces in front of the mirror.
12. Put on a clean pair of pajamas and catch up on your sleep.
13. Get lost in nostalgia and Google all your favorite old movies or TV series, and watch them again to enjoy your time.
14. Alternatively, watch a genre you've never watched before.
15. Start a new show.
16. Organize your music playlist and add new songs.
17. Do some online shopping without breaking your bank account, and leave positive reviews for the purchases or places you love.
18. Create your happy list—write down all the things that make you happy.
19. Make a list of people you are grateful for.

20. Buy yourself some cut flowers and write an appreciative thank-you card to yourself. Keep the flowers where you can see them throughout your workday.

TEN TIPS FOR OVERCOMING FEAR

There is an uncertainty that comes with working remotely that people don't experience as much with in-person jobs. There's less job security, for one; add loneliness for another thing to throw you off kilter. Try these tips for fighting back any fears that may pop up as you transition to your work-at-home lifestyle.

1. **Fear is fueled when you listen to it.** Fear takes over when you forget that you don't have to listen to every thought that pops into your head or out of the mouths of those around you. Be aware when fear is trying to control you—and identify how it keeps you from growing. Understand the beliefs behind your own anxieties and those of other people. Often, the things that scare us are just illusions. Explore whether fear is popping up because of something that happened in the past under very different circumstances. Get in touch with your senses to stay in the present moment: Light a scented candle. Hold an ice cube

with your bare hands. Let a piece of chocolate melt in your mouth. Listen to a meditation or to relaxing music. Look up at the blue sky, and remember where you are right now.

2. **Fear is fueled by inaction.** Sometimes, it takes more energy to do nothing when you are afraid to act than it does to jump into the first step toward overcoming what scares you. Think about jumping off a high dive. If you are afraid of jumping, those moments when you're standing on the ledge with your toes hanging out over the water, feeling every little bounce on the diving board beneath you, are terrifying. The moment you let go of your fear and take the leap, all the fear vanishes, and you begin to *experience* rather than *dread.* Take the first step. Right now.
3. **Fear feeds on indecision.** When we focus too heavily on the outcome of a choice we need to make, our minds get tricked into taking all kinds of paths that may or may not pan out. Imagine that choices are like directions you choose in a maze. If you reach a dead end, you can turn around and try something new. You don't have to know how every decision you make will work out. Part of what makes life spectacular is the element of surprise.
4. **Fear is fueled by the unknown.** When you start to feel fear rise up, give yourself a reality check. Imagine *the worst-case* scenario,

and then ask yourself, "How would I handle that?" Then, imagine *the best-case* scenario, and ask yourself, "How would that feel?" If you can handle the consequences of the worst-case scenario and would feel good with the most positive outcome, chances are, it's just fear messing with your mind.

5. **Fear is fueled by self-doubt.** Instead of thinking, "This is just impossible!" try telling yourself, "Of course this is possible!" Trust that can do anything you set your mind to. If you don't have the skills to achieve something, you can learn them.
6. **Fear is fueled by negative attitudes.** Practice daily affirmations to keep yourself grounded, and talk to people with positive attitudes when you begin to feel doubtful—surround yourself with positive vibes. Look for those who give you good advice. Think, "I can do this!" and "Why not?" instead of "I can't." Don't get trapped into thinking your current situation is all good or all bad. Remember, you are strong and competent. Focus on the good parts of any situation.
7. **Fear is fueled by falsehood.** Don't hide from the facts. Look for the truth in your situation. Remind yourself that many of our fears aren't real, and you aren't the only person in the world who experiences fear. We all have them. Don't be afraid to be afraid. Remember that this is just temporary and completely normal. Fear can't hurt you. It just feels like it can.

8. **Fear is fueled by a lack of breath.** When you start to feel afraid, pay attention to your breathing. Oftentimes, when we are feeling anxious, we start to hyperventilate. If you catch yourself holding your breath or taking short, shallow breaths, take a moment to focus on your breath. Slow down. Take a big deep breath and feel your lungs expand, then exhale slowly through your nose and imagine something that makes you smile. If you can manage it, bust out into deep belly laughter. Learn some coping techniques like meditation or yoga. Keeping a journal will help you also. Write down everything that makes you anxious.
9. **Fear is fueled by your need to be perfect.** We all want to be perfect and to make as few mistakes as possible, but the truth is, we all screw things up and make a mess sometimes. Embrace those messes and screw-ups. They all come with lessons we don't learn unless we try and fail. Avoid harsh judgments, both from others and from yourself. Remember: Making a mess doesn't make *you* a mess.
10. **Fear is fueled by procrastination.** Think of the choices you make in terms of the steps you need to take to complete them. Let's say you have a driving test to pass in the next year, and you are terrified of driving. You won't do yourself any favors by waiting until the evening before the exam to learn how to drive. Take one step today, another tomorrow, and another the next day.

Keep things manageable, so you don't become overwhelmed when you can't procrastinate any longer.

Affirmation: I am a warrior. I am full of courage and strength. Today, I will keep going, despite my fears. I am safe. I can conquer anything. When I step outside my comfort zone and allow myself to face challenges, I grow even stronger than I am right now.

CHANGING YOUR ENVIRONMENT HELPS YOU REMAIN POSITIVE

Choose the color blue. According to research at the University of Sussex in England, surrounding yourself with blue helps calms your mind and improve your mood and ability to concentrate. It increases the speed with which you can complete a task by up to 25 percent and increases your reaction time by 12 percent. It also improves physical performance. Even if you don't live near the beach, or the sky is filled with clouds today, you can surround yourself with blue, which will increase your self-confidence and reduce your stress. See Chapter 2 for other color options.

Listen to upbeat music. If you feel depressed and unmotivated despite the sun shining outside, listening to upbeat music could improve your mood, according to a survey conducted at the University of Missouri. I'm thinking about Pharrell Williams's "Happy." Without a doubt, it soothes my soul when I'm a little sad, tired, or lonely, and I feel in harmony with the world when I listen to it. If you can replace television with music for a while, especially in the morning, that will change everything. Upbeat music will help you concentrate when you need to or let off steam when you're all wound up. It'll relax you when you need it. Listen to upbeat songs that bring pleasant memories and make you dance or sing.

Stop procrastinating. Do the laundry, take out the trash, and mail that envelope for Christ's sakes! Make a to-do list, and avoid letting tasks accumulate. Otherwise, they'll weigh heavily in the back of your mind and spoil all your potential moments of peace and relaxation.

Tidy up. Happiness starts with a pleasant, tidy room. Really. Make your bed; it'll only take a minute, and there's something satisfying and relaxing about it. Also: Don't leave any room empty-handed. Make your trip around the house productive and, when you walk into a room, grab your dirty laundry, put away a dirty mug, and recycle an empty bag. Living in a clean and tidy place brings peace and satisfaction.

Pamper your sense of smell. A pleasant aroma can lift your mood almost immediately (and the opposite is true too). Treat yourself with flowers or scented candles, or get into potpourri making.

Embrace nature. In the United States, a study has shown that walking for one hour among trees can improve memory and attention by 20 percent. In Toronto, researchers have discovered that a fifty-minute daily walk in the wild can treat depression. Outdoor walking strengthens muscles and increases the resistance of the immune system. The breathtaking landscapes, the sounds of nature, being away from the hustle and bustle... all these elements help to stimulate the brain and its creativity. Even if you live in the city, you can still connect with nature: breathe the fresh air, admire the leaves of a nearby tree, try gardening or buy some potted plants, walk barefoot, sunbathe on the balcony, hike, or pick fruit, berries, and wildflowers. In a world that goes faster and faster, it is essential to slow down, and you can do that by finding some peace in nature, which has its own slow jam going on.

Meditate. Regular meditation increases your ability and capacity to feel joy on a daily basis. There is evidence that meditating for a few moments each day helps reduce stress, anxiety, and depression, and therefore makes you happier. By rewiring your brain, meditation allows you to reconnect with yourself, to open yourself to positive things, and to take a step back. You can meditate in the morning to start the day in good mental shape, at lunch to recharge your batteries, or in the evening to get rid of accumulated tension. It's all about finding the right moment. Find a convenient time and an appropriate environment, away from distractions and noise. Plan to wear comfortable and loose clothing.

Minimize. A recent study shows that the desire for material stuff—regardless of whether we acquire the stuff or not—leads to a drop in happiness by negatively affecting our self-esteem and costing us social relationships. James Roberts, director of the study and a marketing professor at Baylor University in Texas, believes that happiness comes from strong relationships with others, and a commitment to our community through volunteer or charitable activities. Various studies confirm that altruism, volunteering, and service—in other words, contributing to the happiness of others—contribute to one's own well-being. Some even conclude that people dedicated to a cause or community organization live longer. Giving money to charities or buying gifts for people you love is good for the soul.

Live in the moment. Most of us have some idea of when or how we will better enjoy life ("When I get this job!" Or "If I get married"), which actually prevents us from being happy, because we're just putting off the joy we could be feeling right now. To think constantly that, if we had acted differently in the past, we would be happier today is just as harmful. The past and the future are largely out of our reach. In order to enjoy yourself right now, stop paying too much attention to what *was* and what *could be*, and learn to take advantage of what's all around you this minute.

Just like the past, the future may be a trap—a source of worry and fear. But sometimes, when things are depressing, a goal can help you move forward: "Okay, it's not going well for now, but if I can get through this bad moment, I know that I can find happiness afterward."

If you aren't living the life you dream of, identify what you can improve, but don't obsess about it. Some things are impossible to control, and there will always be a new problem or a difficult challenge. The best path forward is to believe that everything gets better. From a neuroscientific point of view, there are a host of studies that show that keeping your focus on the present can change brain function in a positive way. The past belongs to the past, and often, it is nostalgia that robs us of our happiness. Yes, yesterday may have been much better than the present, and the future is very scary, but only today matters: the present is all you have, and you will never have anything else. After all, life is a journey, not a destination.

Practice gratitude. Rather than resenting people who have more money or better jobs than you or your family—which lowers self-esteem—try appreciating what you do have. Appreciative people are able to feel real joy when other people do well. Take time to congratulate a person for achieving a goal. When you're having a hard day, think of one thing you're proud you've achieved, and feel the moment of happiness in your heart. Say "thank you," because, no matter what your accomplishments, somebody helped you. Even when it gets rough, find a way to express your gratitude to others and to yourself.

Forgive. We can be very hard on ourselves, but taking responsibility for our actions doesn't mean punishing ourselves. Forgive yourself. People who love themselves learn from their mistakes, accept that everyone makes them, and forgive themselves. It is important that you forgive yourself so you can move forward. How? Remind yourself that you acted in the best possible way in light of the knowledge and level of wisdom you had at the time. Treat yourself kindly—with respect, patience, and gentleness. Also, stop blaming others for what you do not have or how you feel or don't feel. Stop giving up your power and, instead, take responsibility for your life.

Stop complaining. Stop feeling sorry for yourself and thinking about the ways you've failed. Believe in yourself, and don't believe everything your mind says to you, especially if those thoughts are negative or wear you out. Stop complaining about situations, things, and people you can't change. Nobody or nothing can make you unhappy unless you allow it. It's not the situation that triggers these feelings in you, but how you see it. Also, avoid spending too much time with people who are constantly negative. There are many people like this, and even if you like these people, interacting with them may hurt you in the long run. Attitude is as contagious as the flu, so keep yourself protected from bad vibes. Be aware that they are negative, and see them from time to time because you enjoy them, but don't let them rub off on you.

Accept change. Change is the only thing that will allow you to improve your life and the lives of those around you. Do not resist it.

CHECKLIST—REMAIN POSITIVE

- ☐ Choose the color blue.
- ☐ Listen to upbeat music.
- ☐ Stop procrastinating.
- ☐ Tidy up.
- ☐ Pamper your sense of smell.
- ☐ Embrace nature.
- ☐ Meditate.
- ☐ Minimize.
- ☐ Live in the moment.
- ☐ Practice gratitude.
- ☐ Forgive.
- ☐ Stop complaining.
- ☐ Accept change.

USE MOVEMENT AND MUSIC

"How is it that music can, without words, evoke our laughter, our fears, our highest aspirations?"

—**Jane Swan,** history professor and director of the Women's Center at West Chester University of Pennsylvania

Movement and brain health are inherently interconnected, and research suggests that physical exercise is just as beneficial for the brain as it is for the body. Meditative movement has been shown to alleviate depressive symptoms. This is a type of movement in which you pay close attention to your bodily sensations, position in space, and gut feelings (such as subtle changes in heart rate or breathing) as you move. Qigong, tai chi, and some forms of yoga are all helpful for this. Learn new yoga poses and do some sun salutes in your living room. If your children are home with you, try Cosmic Kids Yoga on YouTube (and check out Paige Hodges's book *Yogi Cats* while you're at it). Learn one of Beyoncé's dance routines. Hula hoop! Arm-wrestle! Do twenty push-ups. Build muscle. Stay lean. Get stronger.

The psychological effects of music can also be powerful and wide-ranging. Music therapy is an intervention sometimes utilized to promote emotional health, help patients cope with stress, and boost psychological well-being. Music can relax the mind, energize the body, and even help people better manage pain. Make a new song playlist. Order a disco ball to decorate your living room, and have a family music night. Open a video tutorial and learn some new dance moves. Learn the words to your favorite rap song, or channel your inner poet and write down the most random song ever!

When you are too exhausted to use thought control strategies, such as focusing on the positive or looking at the situation from another angle, movement and music can come to the rescue. Have fun!

My "Cheer Up!" Playlist

____

____

____

My Ultimate Exercise Playlist

____

____

____

My Self-Care Playlist

JOURNAL IT!

Do you have any fitness or other self-care goals? When is your deadline for accomplishing them?

BE CREATIVE

Creativity is a way of living life that embraces originality and makes unique connections between seemingly disparate ideas. Creativity is about living life as a journey into seeing and communicating the extraordinariness of the simplest, most everyday acts. Highly creative people are often seen as rebels and mavericks because they question traditions and rules. Most of us, unfortunately, stifle our creativity as we grow up because society often prizes conformity and inhibits individuality.

Creativity reduces anxiety, depression, and stress. It can also help you process trauma. A creative act such as crafting can help focus the mind and has even been compared to meditation due to its calming effects on the brain and body.

So, start a craft project—make a scrapbook or a family tree, create friendship bracelets or other jewelry that you can either donate or sell, make ombre curtains, or practice origami, the art of paper-folding.

Plant something. Paint a vase or a whole wall pink. Bright pink.

Learn to knit or quilt.

Revamp your old denim jacket and turn it into a chic vest just by cutting its sleeves. Accessorize your old white shirt or jeans with studs or embellishments. Decorate a T-shirt. Make your own Snuggie by hand-stitching a bunch of old sweaters. Dye your T-shirts in the bathtub, alone or with your kids. Spray your shoes with glue and roll them in glitter. Glue crystals onto a pair of sunglasses.

Practice drawing the perfect cat's eye. Write a poem or keep a diary. Make a zine. Make your own bookends. Take a photograph and choose photo editing software to use. Create a couple of photo collages of yourself and your best friends, and design a photo wall in your home.

Create a "theme" lunch for your kids and see if they can guess the theme. Make dinner using only ingredients from the refrigerator or make dinner all one color (spinach pasta with pesto and asparagus).

Decorate your deck or porch. Stick glow-in-the-dark stars all over your ceiling.

Have fun!

TEN TED TALKS TO BOOST YOUR CREATIVITY

TED talks are a great way to motivate yourself and boost creativity, as well as boost your morale if it's sinking. TED hosts some of the most brilliant luminaries from a wide range of industry and career orientations. Most of them are short enough that you can watch them during a lunch break or after hours without taking up a lot of your free time. The following ten TED talks are some of our favorites, but we encourage you to find your own favorites and write them down so you can go back to them whenever you need them.

1. Your Elusive Creative Genius—Elizabeth Gilbert
2. How to Build Your Creative Confidence—David Kelley
3. Four Lessons in Creativity—Julie Burstein
4. Do Schools Kill Creativity?—Ken Robinson
5. We Are the Stories We Tell Ourselves—Shekhar Kapur
6. Success, Failure, and the Drive to Keep Creating—Elizabeth Gilbert

7. The Surprising Habits of Original Thinkers—Adam Grant
8. Embrace the Shake—Phil Hansen
9. Where Does Creativity Hide?—Amy Tan
10. The Power of Vulnerability—Brené Brown

MY OWN TED LIST

FIVE FREE APPS THAT CAN BOOST YOUR CREATIVITY

- Brainsparker is a brainstorming app to help spark creative inspiration.
- SimpleMind. This mind-mapping app will help you connect your ideas into a coherent whole.
- TED Talks. Get ideas and inspiration from the world's leading creative minds.
- Coffitivity recreates the ambient sounds of a cafe. Research shows that such background sounds really do make your brain more creative.
- Unstuck is a self-paced course that teaches you to overcome "stuckness" through provocative questions, targeted tips, and action-oriented tools.

OTHER APPS I WANT TO LOOK INTO

BE CREATIVE: WHAT TO DO WITH EMPTY NOTEBOOKS

Here are some ideas[25] to help you turn your empty journals into beautiful and inspiring works of art as well.

One Sentence a Day | Vision or Mood Boards | Music Journal | Sketchbook | Bullet Journal | Personal Diary | Daily Idea List | Affirmations | Goal Tracker | Date Ideas Diary | Travel Journal | Gratitude Journal | Morning Pages | Prayer Journal | Fitness Tracker | Diet or Calorie Log | Recipes & Meal Planning | To-Do List | Current Events | Bucket List | Sticker Collection | Garden Ideas | Address Book | Password Book | Budget or Savings Tracker | Foreign Language Practice | Dream Home Journal | Fashion Journal | Wedding Planner | Pregnancy Journal | Habit Tracker | Therapy Journal | Astrology Journal | Quote Journal | Creative Writing Prompts | Mind Maps | Write a Novel | Calligraphy Practice | Reading List and Notes | Blog Post Planner | Side Hustle Journal | Movie or TV Show List | Dream Journal | Scrapbook

Primula officinalis

CHAPTER 8

WORK ON YOUR CAREER, YOUR FINANCES—AND YOURSELF

> *"There is nothing noble in being superior to your fellow man; true nobility is being superior to your former self."*
>
> **—Ernest Hemingway**

Part of self-care is making sure that you are professionally and financially stable so you can improve your lot in life. While you're working from home, there are many things you can do in ten minutes or less to improve your career: organize your desk, including all papers and bills; plan your day; read industry news; email someone in your network; share your accomplishments; create your elevator pitch; connect with a mentor and ask questions; read job postings, make a list of your professional goals, and create a plan to achieve those goals; brainstorm your dream job; take a break; and get feedback on your resume after you've updated it on LinkedIn. Check if your finances are in order, create (or adjust) your budget, and devise a debt payoff plan. Google ways to make some side money. Review your retirement options.

And while you're on a kick to improve your career and financial future, work on becoming a well-rounded, all-around better version of yourself. Read a motivating book. Start collecting quotes from successful and inspiring people. Listen to personal growth podcasts. Write down your "perfect self" statement and what you need to do to make it real. Pull out all your old magazines, then cut them up to make a vision board to help you redesign your entire life (you can also use Pinterest). Keep a mindset journal and/or a gratitude list.

When it comes to your career, your finances, and your personal growth, it is usually small things over a long period of time that add up to the success you achieve. Getting into the habit of making small improvements on a daily basis will reap huge rewards over the long run.

The wonderful thing about the worldwide web is that it brings industry professionals closer than a traditional workplace usually can in terms of training, and with that closeness comes the opportunity to learn new life skills and professional development ideas from them. Don't miss out on an opportunity to learn something useful through online training courses. If your situation allows it, request one-on-one coaching.

With a little trial and error, you can create the right amount of structure that allows you to get into a rhythm at home, avoiding distractions, focusing on tasks, and truly excelling in your work.

Go for it!

MONTH AT A GLANCE

Month	
Starting Balance	

Bills

Rent	
Gas/Electric	
Car Payment	
Car Insurance	
Phone	
Internet	
Cable	
Groceries	
Eating Out	

Child Care	
Household	
Personal Care	
Entertainment	
Education	
Clothing	
Gifts	
Medical	
Tithing	

Credit Cards

Other

Budget Goals for Next Month:

Monthly Total

+	Total Income
-	Total Bills
=	

Ending Balance	

YOUR BUDGET CATEGORIES

Budgeting is the first step in your journey to financial freedom. People often go wrong when making a budget by accidentally leaving out categories that will require money at some point. This list is designed to cover as many personal budget categories as possible, but don't be daunted by its size—not all will apply to you, and some you might be more comfortable thinking of as an umbrella category instead of calculating each item individually.

Income	Housing	Food
Salary or wages	Mortgage	Coffee/beverages
Bonus	HELOC	Groceries
Expense reimbursements	Rent	Dining out
Investments	Furnishings	Work food
Dividends and capital gains	Mortgage insurance	School lunch
Interest	Property taxes	Costco membership
Side job income	Repairs and maintenance	Food/grocery delivery service
Gifts	Yard and garden	Alcohol
Tax refund	HOA fees	
Child support		

Utilities	**Transportation**	**Medical/Health**
Cable	Fuel	Doctor
Electricity	Maintenance	Dentist
Water	Registration	Chiropractor
Internet	Repairs	Massage therapist
Garbage	Parking	Hospital
Gas	Tolls	Optometrist
Phone	Fare (public transport)	Prescriptions
		OTC medications/bandages
		Vitamins
		Eyeglasses/hearing aids/ medical devices

Insurance/Taxes	**Savings**	**Giving**
Health Auto Home Life Renters Dental Vision Disability ID theft insurance Umbrella Roadside assistance Taxes and prep fees	Retirement 401(k) IRA Investments College fund Emergency fund	Tithing Charities Specific needs (ex: GoFundMe fundraisers)
Household items Cleaning supplies Laundry supplies Kitchenware Tools	**Education** Tuition Books Fees Field trips Supplies Extracurricular activities (music lessons, school sports) Uniform	**Personal** Salon Makeup Toiletries Grooming (waxes, manicures, etc.) Fitness memberships or equipment Sports Clothing Dry cleaning

Debt Payments Student loan Car loan Credit card Personal loan Hospital bill	**Gifts** Birthday Anniversary Wedding Holiday	**Entertainment and Fun** Games Movies (including Netflix) Vacation Books Music Sporting events Hobbies
Child Care Daycare Camps Babysitter Child support Necessities not accounted for elsewhere (car seat, stroller, diapers)	**Pet care** Food Supplies Vet	**Miscellaneous** Cash (unaccounted for) Office supplies Kids' allowance Safe-deposit box fee

SMART GOALS

Make sure your goals are SMART goals—specific, measurable, attainable, realistic, and time-based. This makes it easier to define and achieve them.

Specific

What exactly do you want to achieve?

Good, achievable goals are clear and defined.

Measurable

How will you know when you've achieved it?

You will need to be able to track daily progress.

Achievable
How can the goal be accomplished?
List the specific tasks you will need to complete.

Relevant
Why is this goal important to you?
Does this goal help add to your plans for the future?

Time-based
When do you want to achieve this goal?
Set your target date so you can guide your work toward a successful completion.

DREAMS AND GOALS

One thing you might consider doing as you shift into a new mindset about your future working from home is to take a month to find more purpose and direction. The following sample calendar can help you target areas of your life you'd like to change and help you better focus on manifesting your ideal future in small steps, one day at a time. We suggest using a journal to reflect on each of these questions—one each day for the next thirty days—and see what transforms for you over the course of a month. You might surprise yourself.

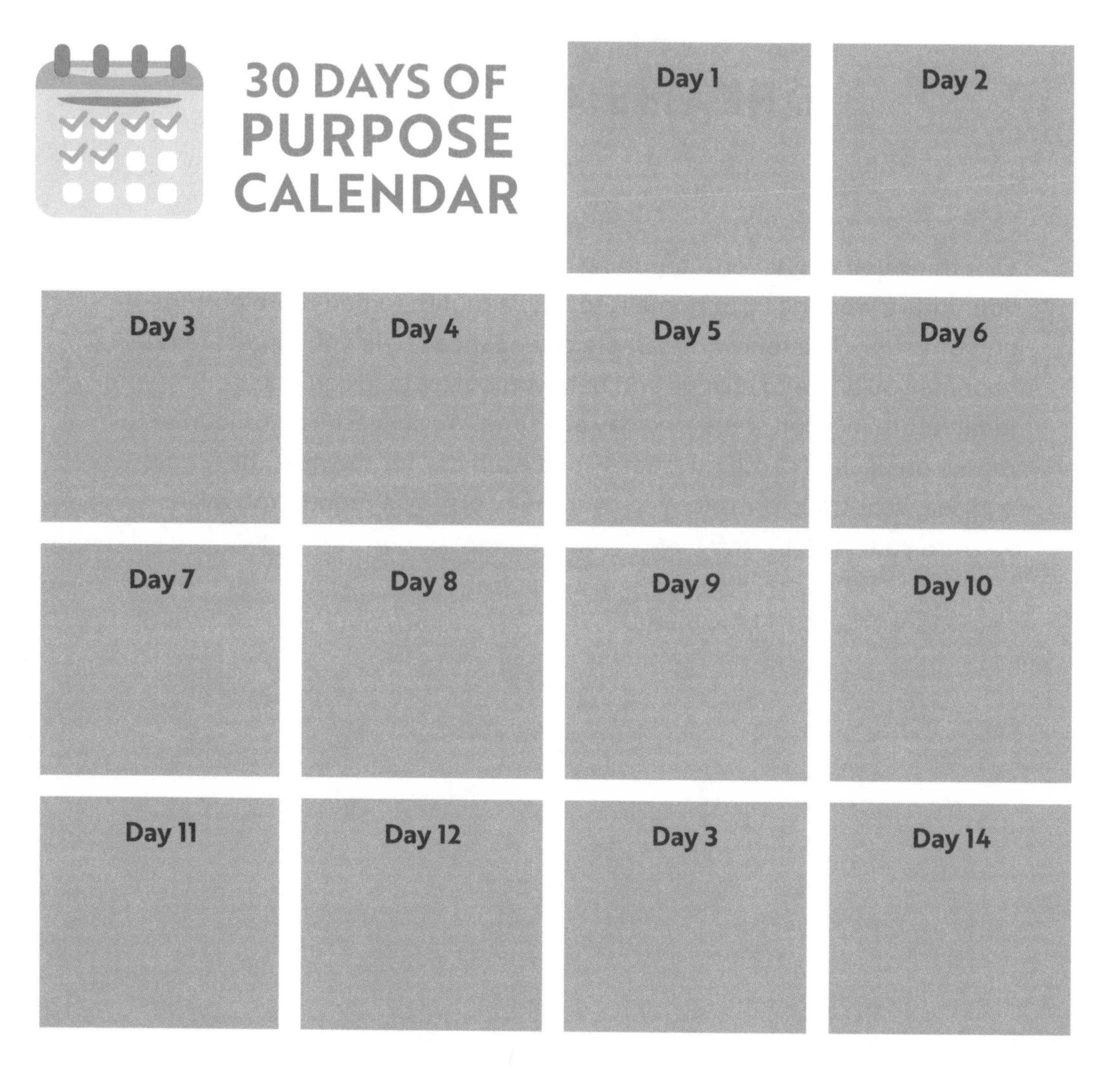
30 DAYS OF PURPOSE CALENDAR
Day 1
Day 2
Day 3
Day 4
Day 5
Day 6
Day 7
Day 8
Day 9
Day 10
Day 11
Day 12
Day 3
Day 14

Day 15	Day 16	Day 17	Day 18
Day 19	Day 20	Day 21	Day 22
Day 23	Day 24	Day 25	Day 26
Day 27	Day 28	Day 29	Day 30

THIRTY DAYS OF PURPOSE

Day 1—In what aspects of your life would you like to make changes?

Day 2—Right this second, what four things are you thankful about?

Day 3—What scares you the most?

Day 4—Are you happy in the house and neighborhood you live in? Why or why not? Where would you most like to live? Don't limit yourself—it could be anywhere in the world!

Day 5—In six months, how much progress would you like to have made? A year? Five years? Ten years? What are you doing to achieve these goals? Write a list of the top ten goals you want to achieve within a year. Make a list of anything that is preventing you from reaching those goals, like distractions or things you don't need to take on to reach them. What in the future worries you the most?

Day 6—Which people in your life are most important to you? How many of the people on your list can you depend on to support you in tough times?

Day 7—What are your personal beliefs? What do you want to accomplish most in life? What do you do that sets you afire? What would make you feel more fulfilled? When do you feel most at peace with yourself?

Day 8—What are the words you use to describe yourself? Are they positive or negative? What ten things do you love most about who you are? Which qualities and talents are you most proud of that require very little effort?

Day 9—What would the perfect day look like to you? What is your dream life? What beliefs hold you back from living that dream life you imagine?

Day 10—Over the past year, what have you discovered is true today that wasn't a year ago?

Day 11—What can you start doing today to make your life easier and less complicated?

Day 12—If you could have a talk with anyone, dead or alive, who would it be? Why? Who are your role models? Why?

Day 13—What is your personal definition of the word "happiness"? What would bring more happiness into your life? Now, think about this one—what robs you of joy? How can you protect your joy?

Day 14—What have been your biggest changes over the past five years? If you could talk to yourself from five years ago, what would you tell him or her?

Day 15—If there was no chance of failure, what would you do? If money was unlimited, what would your ideal life look like? (Where would you choose to live, what career would you pursue, what kind of family would you build?)

Day 16—What did someone do recently to make your day better? How can you make someone else's day better?

Day 17—What life lesson or insight have you gained from a recent challenge? How did going through the darkness and struggle change you into who you are right now?

Day 18—If you knew today was your last day alive, what would you do differently? If you could pick one message you'd want to pass along after you've died, what would it be? How would you like to be remembered?

Day 19—Write a profile of the kind of person you wish to be. Create an avatar for this alternate personality. What are their qualities? Where do they work and live? How do they face difficulties? Write down some ways you can incorporate the qualities your avatar possesses that you don't think you possess.

Day 20—Write out five positive affirmations about yourself. Repeat them daily.

Day 21—What memory brings you the most joy and satisfaction?

Day 22—If you could live during another time period, when would you most want to be alive? What kind of life would you have?

Day 23—Set a two-minute timer, and write down whatever thoughts flash through your mind.

Day 24—What can you do today to bring you closer to achieving your goals?

Day 25—What in life is most important to you? Why?

Day 26—What can you let go of that's holding you back? (Fears, toxic energy, unhealthy relationships?) What bad habits do you need to quit?

Day 27—Draw or paint a picture of something that makes you happy. You can put it in your journal or hang it in your home to remind you to keep your chin up.

Day 28—In what ways do you neglect yourself? How can you start practicing better self-care starting today?

Day 29—What fills you with energy and makes you feel most alive? When was the last time you had that feeling?

Day 30—Make a list of five things you want to try this year that will force you to step out of your comfort zone.

YOUR
WORK
from
HOME
LIFE

CHAPTER 9

DON'T BE AFRAID TO ASK FOR HELP/EXPECT THE UNEXPECTED

When you work from home, not only do the people you work for not see your accomplishments as quickly, they also can't as easily see when you are running into trouble or getting overwhelmed. It's important that you have a team of people you can reach out to in the event that your workload gets to be too much or you just find yourself in over your head. Crisis management teams and virtual assistants are two ways to manage work crises when they do pop up (and they likely will). Building a crisis management team will ensure that any problems are resolved more quickly and efficiently, and a virtual assistant will help keep you focused on priorities.

YOUR CRISIS MANAGEMENT TEAM

Stack your crisis management team with people you know you can rely on if and when things go awry with work. Ask during training who you need to contact to resolve different kinds of issues that might pop up. It's smart to ask during your training and orientation for clarity on who handles what at your company. The following template should help you keep their contact information in a handy place where it can be accessed quickly.

- Name
- Phone number
- Email
- Role

As a remote worker, there'll come a time when it'll be impossible to do everything yourself, at least well enough to be efficient and effective. A virtual assistant is a person who provides support services to other businesses from a remote location.

TEN THINGS TO OUTSOURCE TO A VIRTUAL ASSISTANT[26]

- Bookkeeping
- Online research
    - Doing research based on the instructions
    - Searching for guest blog opportunities
    - Keeping an eye on competitors
    - Searching for new business opportunities with the help of the internet
    - Searching for best practices in your business domain
- Database entries
    - Database building and updating (sales, contacts, CRM, etc.)
    - Reviewing data for accuracy
    - Generating reports and entering data into CRM
    - Compiling data collected from online surveys and entering it into CRM
- Data presentations (preparing slideshows, PowerPoint presentations)

- Managing email and setting up autoresponders through Aweber or Mailchimp
- Social tasks
- Receptionist duties (answering occasional calls)
- Personal errands
- Social media tasks:
    - Creating Facebook, LinkedIn pages for your business
    - Creating profiles on various social channels, such as Twitter, Tumblr, YouTube, etc.
    - Updating the latest information on your social profiles
    - Finding relevant content to share on your social channels
    - Managing, building the relevant audience on different social channels
    - Monitoring engagement on your social network
    - Measuring analytics on different social profiles
    - Managing blogs
    - Participation in discussion forums (more promotion!)
- Travel research
- Hotel and flight bookings
- Scheduling

- Calendar management
- Chasing business
- Recruitment (for new team members like writers or graphic artists)
- Industry knowledge prep
- Liaison with other team members
- E-commerce tasks
    - Writing SEO-friendly product descriptions
    - Product category management
    - Editing product images
    - Order processing
    - Handling exchange and return via phone, chat, emails
    - Conducting competitor analysis
    - Handling transaction on your website
    - Offering customer support
    - Commenting on reviews
- Administrative tasks
    - Email managing/labeling
    - Creating basic reports
    - Transcription duties (from audio, video, podcasts, etc.)
    - Taking minutes from meetings

- Booking appointments with clients
- Following up with clients and customers
- Calendar management
- File management with the help of Dropbox
- Answering support tickets
- Writing and sending invoices to your customers
- Producing graphs from your spreadsheets

The following worksheets will help guide your research on virtual assistants.

How to Hire a Virtual Assistant (Tip)	Source	Notes

Pros of a Virtual Assistant	Source	Notes

Cons of a Virtual Assistant	Source	Notes

What I Need Help With:

WATCH YOUR BACK: BACKING UP DATA AND CRITICAL RECORDS

Technology is prone to breakdowns at the most inconvenient times. Let's say you're almost done with that quarterly report, and the power goes out. When it comes back on, you boot up your computer and frantically try to find traces of the hard work you've put in over the past week, to no avail. Losing documents or data can be frustrating at the very least, and in some cases career-wrecking. Learn how to back up your work frequently to avoid a catastrophic loss. Here are six ways we back up our work:

SIX WAYS TO BACK UP YOUR DATA

1. USB sticks
2. External hard drive
3. Time machine
4. Network attached storage
5. Cloud storage
6. Printing

BE PREPARED

"Life can only be understood backward; but it must be lived forward."
—Søren Kierkegaard

While, hopefully, things will remain calm and peaceful, every once in a while, a state of emergency happens, and, as someone who works from home, you'll need to be prepared for that eventuality. M.J. grew up in Port-au-Prince, Haiti—a place of civil unrest and violent demonstrations—and her most vivid childhood memories from the late eighties involve a state of siege that empowered the National Palace to deny the right of assembly and to impose curfews. Schools were closed and businesses shut down after anti-government protests, and heavily armed "Tontons Macoutes" and steel-helmeted soldiers in olive-drab uniforms patrolled the streets in a show of force. While part of her was terrified, another was exhilarated, because it meant storytelling time with her father, baking with her mother, and arts and crafts with her sister. Everyone was forced to remain home, and it could be magical to put aside the chaos and violence outside and live in a sort of separate peace.

Now that she's "adulting" (in America), with mounting deadlines and a jam-packed schedule, being homebound (whether because of a hurricane, a snow day, or a quarantine) can present many complex issues and complications beyond having enough food and supplies for weeks at a time.

In March 2020, "social distancing" became a key phrase around the world, as cities and towns everywhere confronted the growing number of COVID-19 cases. Public health officials asked that we limit close contact with other individuals in order to avoid catching the virus or passing it on. Concerts were canceled and theaters closed, museums shut their doors, and workers were told to stay home to prevent infection. The situation—confused and uncertain—brought back memories of Port-au-Prince and her days in isolation.

Isolation gets tough—emotionally—and may bring fear and worry about our own health and the health of our loved ones; changes in our sleep or eating patterns; difficulty sleeping or concentrating; the worsening of chronic health problems; and an increased use of alcohol, tobacco, or other drugs.

A homebound situation can be downright terrifying.

We should always be prepared for emergencies ranging from self-isolation to full-blown quarantine to weeks of power interruptions and municipal water shutdowns or boil advisories. Make a plan for these stressful situations (what to do? where to go? who to call?). Put together an emergency kit. If in isolation, shop for all useful things online. Read the news. Do a maintenance tour of your home, clean appliances, and check whether anything needs fixing (or updating once social distancing is over).

But also be prepared for your return to normalcy.

Fresh starts feel good! Put your camera in your handbag, so you don't forget to take pictures when you finally get to leave the house. Research and plan a road trip to ensue as soon as your self-imposed cabin fever is over. Lament the small number of stamps in your passport and resolve to up your international playgirl/playboy game. Plan your dream vacation.

Go on! Start planning—and purchasing—birthday and holiday gifts for your favorite people. Plan a family or friend meet-up. Looking toward the future will keep you in a good mood.

BE PREPARED: BASIC EMERGENCY SUPPLY KIT

A basic emergency supply kit could include the following recommended items:

- ☐ Water—one gallon of water per person per day for at least three days, for drinking and sanitation
- ☐ Food—at least a three-day supply of nonperishable food
- ☐ Battery-powered or hand-crank radio and a NOAA Weather Radio with tone alert
- ☐ Flashlight
- ☐ First aid kit
- ☐ Extra batteries
- ☐ Whistle to signal for help
- ☐ Dust mask to help filter contaminated air and plastic sheeting, and duct tape to shelter-in-place
- ☐ Moist towelettes, garbage bags, and plastic ties for personal sanitation

- ☐ Wrench or pliers to turn off utilities
- ☐ Manual can opener for food
- ☐ Local maps
- ☐ Cell phone with chargers and a backup battery

ADDITIONAL EMERGENCY SUPPLIES

Consider adding the following items to your emergency supply kit based on your individual needs:

- ☐ Prescription medications
- ☐ Nonprescription medications such as pain relievers, anti-diarrhea medication, antacids, or laxatives
- ☐ Glasses and contact lenses solution
- ☐ Infant formula, bottles, diapers, wipes, diaper rash cream
- ☐ Pet food and extra water for your pet
- ☐ Cash or traveler's checks
- ☐ Important family documents such as copies of insurance policies, identification, and bank account records saved electronically or in a waterproof, portable container
- ☐ Sleeping bag or warm blanket for each person

- ☐ Complete change of clothing appropriate for your climate and sturdy shoes
- ☐ Household chlorine bleach and medicine dropper to disinfect water
- ☐ Fire extinguisher
- ☐ Matches in a waterproof container
- ☐ Feminine supplies and personal hygiene items
- ☐ Mess kits, paper cups, plates, paper towels, and plastic utensils
- ☐ Paper and pencil
- ☐ Books, games, puzzles, or other activities for children

JOURNAL IT!

Imagine the power has gone out and there's no running water in your home. Officials announce it may be weeks before power and plumbing are restored. How would you handle this situation? What about your company, what do they do in the event of a major catastrophic event? What would you do? What steps have you taken to ensure you have an evacuation plan in place?

Where would you go and what would you do there? Be sure to include the sights, smells, and sounds of the setting to give your piece a strong sense of place.

WHAT ABOUT ALTRUISM AND GRATITUDE? WAYS TO HELP DURING A CRISIS

"Every man must decide whether he will walk in the light of creative altruism or in the darkness of destructive selfishness."
—Martin Luther King, Jr.

BE GENEROUS. You can help during a crisis.

- The homeless, elderly, and hungry will need your help. Donate to charities that support them, such as Meals on Wheels, Save the Children, The Center for Disaster Philanthropy, and your local food bank, which may be struggling with fewer donations and unable to get some staples due to stockpiling.
- Do not let food go to waste. According to Feeding America, each year, 72 billion pounds of food goes to waste. A few simple ways to cut down on food waste include "storing food in the proper place (and at the proper temperature), waiting to wash produce until

you're ready to use it (to avoid mold), freeze anything that you don't expect to use in the near future (if freezing is possible), make a stock, compost, and for crying out loud, eat your leftovers!"

- Support the arts by making a donation to your favorite museum or local arts organization. Many organizations were forced to interrupt programming and close their doors. Whether they're on the front lines of the fight to quell the coronavirus, or their mission is entirely unrelated to the current crisis, your dollars will make a big difference.
- Buy from small businesses; they struggle when people are staying home.
- Donate blood. When people stay home, blood donations are expected to fall, and the Red Cross will still need lots of donors.
- If you are not vulnerable, check in on others, particularly elderly neighbors who might need something picked up from the store. Because self-isolation can be very lonely, offer to Skype or Zoom with others.
- Call your senator and ask them to approve paid sick leave and paid family leave.
- Speak up against xenophobia and racism. During the coronavirus outbreak, there was a lot of prejudice against Asian-Americans and Pacific Islanders. The Centers for Disease Control (CDC) posted

this message on its "Share Facts Not Fear" website: "People of Asian descent, including Chinese-Americans, are not more likely to get COVID-19 than any other American. Help stop fear by letting people know that being of Asian descent does not increase the chance of getting or spreading COVID-19."

- Manage your own anxiety and stress.
- Be responsible: In case of an outbreak, keep your distance, wash your hands, and stay informed. Stop the spreading of false information and rumors. Ensuring that you're making safe and smart choices is a civic duty of the utmost importance.

OTHER WAYS TO VOLUNTEER

JOURNAL IT!

Where would you like to volunteer? How do you currently give back to your community?

BONUS CHAPTER

GRATITUDE

In addition to planning, budgeting, and so on, *Your Work from Home Life* has also focused on ways to love yourself, because working from home requires a lot of self-care and self-improvement.

One way to foster self-improvement is to practice gratitude.

When you practice being thankful for what you have and those who helped you along the way, you become more upbeat, more confident, more efficient, less stressed, less jealous of other people, and more satisfied with your life.

HERE ARE TEN EXERCISES TO BRING GRATITUDE INTO YOUR LIFE:

Three good things: This is one of the easiest and best-known exercises to practice gratitude. Every night before going to bed, take a few minutes to think back over the day that has just passed. Focus on positive events, then find three things you can be thankful for. This exercise will be particularly useful after a tough day, because it will help you remember the positive parts of your day, even if the whole day felt like a nightmare, or you think you made one mistake after another. Maybe, even though you woke up a half-hour late and had to skip breakfast, you still managed to start work on time. Maybe you sprained your ankle at the gym, but you were helped out by other people who showed you how much they care about you. There's usually something positive to be found in any situation. It might take some digging to find it, but you can do it!

You will find that you can still find positives: a pleasant discussion with a neighbor, a free spot in a crowded parking lot, your baby sister who ran into your arms when she returned from kindergarten, a delicious meal, a postcard from the other side of the world...there are always reasons to feel happy.

Remember to thank life for these little gifts, these little pleasures. You can also do this exercise when you wake up or at breakfast time, but what a happy way to fall asleep, with your heart filled with joy and gratitude.

The gratitude journal or gratitude book: Take a notebook and a pen and, for the first exercise, think back over your day. This time, note three to five things you can give thanks for once a day, once or more a week. Find a comfortable pace so this is an ongoing commitment. Completing your gratitude journal should be a pleasure, not a chore. Put it on your nightstand and fill it when you feel like it.

If you prefer new technologies, another variation of the gratitude journal is to take pictures of things you feel grateful for. You can try the experience over a week by taking a picture a day, for example. You can also test apps like *Gratitude Journal 365* or *HappyFeed—Gratitude Journal*. Another possibility: make these images into a beautiful collage you can hang on your wall to keep the things you are thankful for on your mind.

The letter of gratitude: This is a powerful exercise in giving thanks and showing appreciation to others. Write a letter to someone who matters tremendously to you—someone who has inspired you or currently inspires you to be as badass as you are, but who you have not yet taken the time or the trouble to thank. It can be a teacher, a mentor, a parent, a grandparent, a friend, a coworker, or anyone else. Someone who has helped you, who inspires you, who has shown kindness or generosity, or someone you can rely on, that you are genuinely grateful to have in your life. In short, someone toward whom you genuinely feel appreciation and gratitude.

You don't need to write a novel, unless you want to. Be specific about what that person has done for you and how they made your life better. If they've been a role model, point out the qualities you appreciate in them. Explain to them what fills you with gratitude. You can choose a handwritten version that's more personal, and scan and email it. However you go about doing it, it's important to let people who lift you up know that you appreciate the difference they've made in your life.

The gratitude e-visit: If you aren't shy about showing your feelings, one step above the letter of gratitude is the e-visit of gratitude. Instead of sending your letter, you make an online appointment with the rock stars in your life and read it in person. Tell them you want to meet to discuss something, but don't mention the letter of gratitude. Stay vague. Keep this a surprise.

When you are in front of the person, tell them that you want to read a letter describing how thankful you are to them. Ask them not to interrupt you until you have finished reading your letter. Take your time. As you read, try to pay attention to the reactions of the recipient, but also pay attention to your own.

At the end of the reading, discuss your feelings—this exercise often brings up strong emotions. If you live far away from this person, new technologies can make it easier. You can have a video chat over Skype, Google Hangouts, or social networks.

The jar of gratitude: To create your jar of gratitude, you will need paper, a pen, a jar, and whatever decorations you think will reflect your personality:

stickers, paint, glitter, ribbons, glue, etc. Then decorate it. Make this a jar that fills your heart with joy when you look at it. Once your jar is ready, place it in a room where you are sure to see it every day. Ideally, choose a place where you spend the end of the day: if you put it in the bathroom, you will see it when you brush your teeth or, if you place it on your bedside table, you can look at it before going to bed.

Then, as you did in the exercise above, practice thinking about three events of your day for which you feel grateful. It can be small pleasures like tasting your favorite pastry, receiving a call from your best friend, or enjoying a beautiful sunset. Every day, note these moments of happiness on slips of paper and place them in your jar of gratitude. As your jar fills up, you will realize that you have plenty of reasons to be grateful. If you ever feel a little down, open your jar and pull out some memories to remind yourself it ain't all that bad.

Some people prefer to put a coin in their jar of gratitude whenever they feel grateful. Then, once filled, you can donate it to a cause you want to help out.

The gratitude box: As with the jar of gratitude, get a box and anything you think is necessary to make it pretty. This time, the exercise involves writing messages of gratitude to the person of your choice. If you're out of inspiration for ways people have helped you out, you can thank people for some of the special qualities that make them unique, write down things you like about this person, what they taught you, how they inspire you, and just say thanks for being part of your life.

Here are some examples:

> Thank you for your patience at the doctor's office | Your kindness touches me so much | Thank you for your kindness to me | Thank you for being here for me, I'm so lucky to have a friend like you | What I like about you is that you always believe in me | Thank you for supporting me and encouraging me with all my projects | I like to talk about how life is going with you. It makes me feel like I can do better | Thank you for being yourself | I love you as you are

Open your heart, and let your feelings speak! Fill your box of gratitude with all your little words, and offer it up on a special occasion. I think it's a wonderful gift idea for Valentine's Day, a loved one's birthday, a teacher, Father's Day or Mother's Day, or even Christmas.

The gratitude walk: This exercise of gratitude couldn't be simpler. It combines the benefits of physical activity, gratitude, and mindfulness meditation. Go for a walk, somewhere where you are close to nature if possible. Walk slowly and focus on the present moment. Pay attention to all the wonders that surround you, everything that can give you pleasure, and what you are grateful for in this moment. It may be, for example, the song of birds, the beauty of butterflies, the color of trees, the smell of flowers, the wind in your hair, the heat of the sun on your skin... Let yourself be overwhelmed by this deep sense of well-being and gratitude. Allow yourself at least twenty to thirty minutes of walking. This is the time your body needs to secrete feel-good endorphins. The practice of regular physical activity has a positive impact on your morale, your level of stress, and the quality of your sleep. In addition to allowing you to express your gratitude, this exercise is perfect for clearing your head of your worries and anxieties.

Gratitude meditation: Here's another exercise that combines meditation and gratitude, two activities that help elevate your level of happiness. To practice a gratitude meditation, sit comfortably in a place where you know you won't be disturbed. Close your eyes and focus on your breathing. Let all your cares out as you exhale stress and drama, and breathe in peace. Breathe deeply until you reach a state of calm. Pay attention to things around you that you can hear or feel: the breeze on your skin, the birds in the trees, the traffic in the distance, the rush of water, whatever is in the place you are at—and say inwardly, "For all this, I am grateful."

Next, think about the important people in your life: your family members, your friends, your boyfriend/girlfriend or spouse, your kids... Soak up the love and gratitude you feel for them, and in the same way, say, "thank you," inwardly. "For all these people, I am grateful." Mentally review the things that make you grateful for life, not forgetting what we tend to take for granted, such as the chance to be alive and healthy, our ability to see, hear, walk, and communicate, You can also visualize the physical things you have—such as technology—and how they make your life easier. Take the necessary time: two, five, ten, or even fifteen minutes, and give thanks.

The gratitude inventory: List a hundred things that you are grateful for. Yes, one hundred things. I know, at first, it may seem impossible to find that many, but they are there. If it helps, create categories: your possessions, your relationship, the activities you enjoy, your current job or your previous jobs, your qualities and traits, outings, concerts, trips you've made, and all the places you've visited, your health, and that of your loved ones, all your life experiences you are proud of, awards that you have received, sports or academic achievements, or organizations you belong to. Think about your interests. For example, if you're interested in entertainment, you could think about someone you met who you admire, like a recording artist or an actress you're a big fan of. Maybe you went to a concert where the tickets sold out quickly. Maybe you've won a contest or prize money. Once you get started, you'll find that you will fill your gratitude inventory with a lot more ease than you thought.

The gratitude stone: We get so wrapped up in the routine of everyday life that it's not always easy to think of practicing gratitude spontaneously, let alone regularly. Here is a little exercise that can help you. Choose a rock or a small stone that you like, regardless of its appearance. The stone here is nothing but a symbol, a physical object whose purpose is to remind you to practice gratitude. You can just as easily replace it with any other small object that means gratitude to you. Put your stone of gratitude in your pocket, in your purse, or leave it out on your desk. Choose a place where you are sure you can see it all day long, whenever you want to. Whenever you see it or touch it, if it's in your pocket, take a break and think of at least one thing for which you feel gratitude or joy right then, at that very moment. Another technique is to program one or more alarms on your phone. For example, one when you get up in the morning and one in the evening at bedtime. If you use this method, remember the positive events that occurred between the two alarms. Feel and express your gratitude.

THIRTY DAYS OF GRATITUDE

---

1. What does gratitude mean to you?
2. What does "the grass is always greener on the other side" mean to you? What are you taking for granted that you should be thankful for?
3. Write about a happy memory.
4. Write about a place you've been to that you're grateful for.
5. What's something you're grateful to have today that you didn't have a year ago? Write a letter or note to your older self, and list five things you'll be grateful for when you reach her age.
6. What's a simple pleasure that you're grateful for?
7. What's something about your body or health that you're grateful for?
8. Look around the room and write about everything you see that you're grateful for. Then, open the door or window and look outside. What's something you're grateful for outside? What are you thankful for in nature?

9. What's an accomplishment you're proud of? What skill(s) do you have that you're grateful for?
10. What mistake or failure are you grateful for?
11. What's a possession that makes your life easier?
12. Open your phone or photo album and find a photo that you like. Why are you grateful for this photo?
13. What have you been given that you're grateful for?
14. What public service or organization are you grateful for (e.g., the library or fire department)?
15. What book(s) are you grateful for?
16. What piece of clothing or furniture are you grateful for?
17. List three things that made you smile today.
18. Recall a time when you needed and received encouragement.
19. What is a luxury you are thankful for?
20. What's a tradition you're grateful for?
21. What's one of your personality traits that you're grateful for?
22. What's something you made recently that you're grateful for?
23. What will show your family you are grateful for them today?
24. Why are you grateful for your country?

25. What are the lyrics from a song that inspires you?
26. What's something that you bought recently that you're grateful for?
27. What is the most unexpected compliment you ever got?
28. What time of day are you grateful for?
29. What is one scent you're grateful for?
30. Who are you grateful for? It could be a friend, a teacher or mentor, a family member, or anyone else in your life who makes you feel safe. It could even be an artist, an author, or a musician.

CONCLUSION

YOU HAVE THE KEYS

You have all the keys you need to be a success! Once you start using the suggestions you found in this book and are working from home, you'll better understand how little positive habits can bring feelings of well-being to you as well as those you work with. Working from home isn't hard if you create the ideal environment to work in, set boundaries, manage distractions, plan well, and take the time to make sure your household runs in a way that supports your career goals.

The exercises and lists in this book are all tools that will make working from home more manageable. You don't have to practice them all, but do try them out to find the ones that work for you. You'll know which ones are effective, because they'll bring you the most efficiency, happiness, and satisfaction. New technologies and applications are being built with more frequency, so stay abreast of upcoming innovations and learn to be flexible.

Choose to do these on a schedule that suits you, but remember, regular practice and training will help you see results much faster than randomly reaching for one when you're desperate for a boost. Of course, this is also the field guide to reach for in times of desperation, but make it part of your routine to reap the biggest benefits.

Working from home can be a difficult path, but it can also bring a great deal of personal satisfaction. Part of finding the joy in working from home is understanding that your mindset is key to your success.

We wish you all the best in your new career path!

ABOUT THE AUTHORS

Born in Port-au-Prince, Haiti, **M.J. Fievre** moved to the United States in 2002. She currently writes from Miami, Florida. M.J.'s publishing career began as a teenager in Haiti. At nineteen years-old, she signed her first book contract with Hachette-Deschamps, in Haiti, for the publication of a Young Adult book titled *La Statuette Maléfique*. Since then, M.J. has written nine books in French that are widely read in Europe and the French Antilles. In 2013, One Moore Book released M.J.'s first children's book, *I Am Riding*, written in three languages: English, French, and Haitian Creole. In 2015, Beating Windward Press published M.J.'s memoir, *A Sky the Color of Chaos*, about her childhood in Haiti during the brutal regime of Jean-Bertrand Aristide. She is also the author of *Happy, Okay? Poems about Anxiety, Depression, Hope, and Survival* and *Empowered Black Girl: Joyful Affirmations and Words of Resilience*. A long-time educator and frequent keynote speaker, M.J. is available for book club meetings, podcast presentations, interviews and other author events.

Becca Anderson comes from a long line of teachers and preachers from Ohio and Kentucky. The teacher side of her family led her to become a woman's studies scholar and the author of the bestselling *The Book of*

Awesome Women. An avid collector of affirmations, meditations, prayers, and blessings, she helps run a "Gratitude and Grace Circle" that meets monthly at homes, churches, and bookstores in the San Francisco Bay Area where she currently resides. Becca Anderson credits her spiritual practice and daily prayer with helping her recover from cancer and wants to share this encouragement with anyone who is facing difficulty in life with *Prayers for Hard Times* and her latest, *The Woman's Book of Prayer.* The author of *Think Happy to Stay Happy* and *Every Day Thankful,* Becca Anderson shares prayers and affirmations, inspirational writings and suggested acts of kindness at thedailyinspoblog.wordpress.com She also blogs about Awesome Women at theblogofawesomewomen.wordpress.com/ @AndersonBecca_ on Twitter @BeccaAndersonWriter on Facebook @BeccaAndersonWriter on Instagram

OUR KICK-ASS REFERENCE LIST

1 **Know What You're Signing Up For: Questions to Ask Yourself.**

RWH Editor. "21 Questions to Ask a Remote Employee at Interview." remoteworkhub.com/20-questions-ask-remote-employer-interview/.

2 **Know What You're Signing Up For: Questions to Ask Your Employer / Questions to Ask Yourself.**

Browning, Randle. "Want a Remote Job? 18 Interview Questions You Need to Answer." skillcrush.com/blog/remote-job-interview-questions.

Lighthouse Editor. "31 Questions to Ask Remote Employees to Better Support Them." getlighthouse.com/blog/questions-remote-employees.

3 **Create Your Workspace: Tips to Set-Up Your Workspace.**

Duffy, Jill. "Everything You Need to Set Up an Ergonomic Home Office." www.pcmag.com/how-to/everything-you-need-to-set-up-an-ergonomic-home-office.

Pelta, Rachel. "How to Set Up a Home Office You Love: 12 Tips." www.flexjobs.com/blog/post/setting-up-home-office-v2.

Rogers, Marilyn. "8 Tips to Set Up Your Home Office for Productivity." www.lifehack.org/369556/8-tips-set-your-home-office-for-serious-productivity.

4 **Create Your Workspace: Best Colors for Productivity.**

Genever, Harriet. "4 Colors that Give You an Unexpected Productivity Boost." redbooth.com/hub/colors-unexpected-productivity-boost.

Shandrow, Kim Lachance. "How the Color of Your Office Impacts Productivity (Infographic)." www.entrepreneur.com/article/243749.

5 **Create Your Workspace: The Essential List of Office Supplies for your Home Office.**

Free Pintable Home Office Supply List. www.home-storage-solutions-101.com/home-office-supplies.html.

Pilon, Annie. "The Definitive Office Supplies Checklist for Small Businesses." smallbiztrends.com/2018/12/office-supplies-checklist-small-business.html.

6 **Setting Up Your Virtual Office: The List of Essential Apps.**

Brooks, Aaron. "10 Best Apps for Working Remotely from Home." www.ventureharbour.com/best-apps-working-remotely-from-home.

Zapier Editorial Team. "Work from Home Apps." zapier.com/blog/work-from-home-apps/.

7 **Book Recommendation.**

Hanna, Heidi. Stressaholic. Wiley, 2014.

8 **Peak Hours: The "Getting Started" Routine for Your Work from Home Life.**

Bradberry, Travis. "11 Tips to Transform Your Morning Routine and Make Your Entire Day More Productive." www.success.com/11-tips-to-transform-your-morning-routine-and-make-your-entire-day-more-productive/.

Brown, Lachlan. "12 Tips for a Perfect Morning Routine (According to Science)." hackspirit.com/morning-routine.

Ho, Leon. "50 Ways to Increase Productivity and Achieve More in Less Time." www.lifehack.org/articles/featured/50-ways-to-increase-your-productivity.html.

Lee, Kevan. "The Morning Routines of the Most Successful People." www.fastcompany.com/3033652/the-morning-routines-of-the-most-successful-people.

Loder, Vanessa. "5 Best To-Do List Tips." www.forbes.com/sites/vanessaloder/2014/06/02/five-best-to-do-list-tips/#5d9119ee651b.

Rampton, John. "15 Ways to Increase Productivity at Work." www.inc.com/john-rampton/15-ways-to-increase-productivity-at-work.html.

Rampton, John. "101 Time Management Tips to Boost Productivity Every Day." www.entrepreneur.com/article/318566.

9 **Book Recommendation. Allen, David. Getting Things Done.**

10 **The End of Day Routine.**

Fetters, K. Aleisha. "6 Tips to Build a Better Bedtime Routine." time.com/4366736/6-tips-for-bedtime-routine.

Khidekel, Marina. "19 Powerful Nighttime Routines that Will Help You Wake Up Happy." thriveglobal.com/stories/happy-nighttime-routines.

11 **Take a Break: The Basic Rules.**

Duffy, Jill. "How to Take Better Breaks to Boost Your Productivity." www.pcmag.com/how-to/get-organized-how-to-take-better-breaks-to-boost-your-productivity.

Seiter Courtney. "The Science of Taking Breaks at Work." open.buffer.com/science-taking-breaks-at-work.

12 **Take a Break.**

Shih, Jenny. "How to Take Breaks When You've Got Too Much to Do." www.fastcompany.com/90302847/the-best-ways-to-take-a-break-at-work.

13 **Take a Break.**

Duffy, Jill. "How to Take Better Breaks to Boost Your Productivity." www.pcmag.com/how-to/get-organized-how-to-take-better-breaks-to-boost-your-productivity.

14 **Take a Break.**

"100 Productive Things to Do in PJs." And girlvsglobe.com/100-productive-things-to-do.

Bridges, Frances. "The Most Productive Ways to Take a Break at Work." www.forbes.com/sites/francesbridges/2018/09/29/most-productive-ways-to-take-breaks/#6d40e7826f9b.

Rampton, John. "101 Time Management Tips to Boost Productivity Every Day." www.entrepreneur.com/article/318566.

Seiter Courtney. "The Science of Taking Breaks at Work." open.buffer.com/science-taking-breaks-at-work.

The Muse Editor. "Take Five: 51 Things to Do When You Need a Break at Work." www.themuse.com/advice/take-five-51-things-to-do-when-you-need-a-break-at-work.

15 **Understand the Basics of Planning and Scheduling.**

Beard, Catherine. "How to Plan Your Weekly Schedule for Success." theblissfulmind.com/how-to-plan-your-week.

Kendrick, Tonia. "Dramatically Improve the Way You Plan Your Day." solopreneurdiaries.com/how-to-plan-your-day.

Matthews, Kayla. "How to Plan Your Entire Week Under 30 Minutes: 8 Productivity Tips That Work." www.makeuseof.com/tag/plan-week-productivity.

Rampton, John. "101 Time Management Tips to Boost Productivity Every Day." www.entrepreneur.com/article/318566.

Robbins, Tony. "Planning Your Workday for Success." www.tonyrobbins.com/importance-time-management/how-to-plan-your-day.

Scalco, Dan. "5 Tips to Organize Your Day for Maximum Productivity." www.huffpost.com/entry/productivity-tips_b_7608084.

16 **Set Boundaries Between Home and Work When Work is at Home: The Perfect Work-Life Balance.**

Lee, Deborah Jian. "6 Tips for Better Work-Life Balance." www.forbes.com/sites/deborahlee/2014/10/20/6-tips-for-better-work-life-balance/#717e238b29ff.

Patel, Sujan. "Adopt These 12 Habits for a Better Work-Life Balance" www.entrepreneur.com/article/247563.

Sanfilippo, Marisa. "How to Improve Your Work-Life Balance Today." www.businessnewsdaily.com/5244-improve-work-life-balance-today.html.

The Muse Editor. "37 Tips for a Better Work-Life Balance." www.themuse.com/advice/37-tips-for-a-better-worklife-balance.

17 **Set Boundaries Between Home and Work When Work is at Home: 15 Ways to Avoid Distractions.**

Daskal, Lolly. "10 Smart Tips to Prevent Distractions and Sharpen Your Focus." www.inc.com/lolly-daskal/10-smart-tips-to-prevent-distractions-and-sharpen-your-focus.html.

Lane, Andrea. "12 Tips for Staying Focus and Avoiding Diistraction at Work." redbooth.com/hub/12-tips-for-staying-focused-and-avoiding-distraction-at-work.

Mires, Ericson Ay. "How to Not Get Distracted: 10 Practical Tips to Sharpen Your Focus." www.lifehack.org/articles/productivity/10-critical-tips-prevent-distraction-and-sharpen-your-focus.html.

Zipkin, Nina. "11 Ways to Avoid Distractions and Stay Focused." www.entrepreneur.com/video/240176.

18 **Set Boundaries Between Home and Work When Work is at Home: 6 Ways to Avoid the Social Media Temptation.**

"15 Easy Ways to Disconnect from Social Media and the Internet." www.thegal-ivanter.com/blog/how-to-disconnect-break-internet-phones-productivity.

Cavoulacos, Alex. "13 Ways for the Chronically Connected to Disconnect." www.forbes.com/sites/dailymuse/2013/12/12/13-ways-for-the-chronically-connected-to-disconnect/#2463fd864194.

19 **Set Boundaries Between Home and Work When Work is at Home: How to Deal with Time and Energy Vampires.**

Chua, Celestine. "How to Deal with Energy Vampires: 8 Simple Tips." personalexcellence.co/blog/energy-vampires.

DiGiulio, Sarah. "How to Stop (and Deal With) an Energy Vampire." www.nbcnews.com/better/health/how-spot-deal-energy-vampire-ncna896251.

Frost, Aja. "21 Ways to Leave a Never-Ending Conversation Without Being Rude." www.themuse.com/advice/21-ways-to-leave-a-neverending-conversation-without-being-rude.

Walpole, Dani. "6 Polite Ways to End a Conversation." www.rd.com/advice/relationships/polite-ways-to-end-a-conversation.

20 **Set Boundaries Between Home and Work When Work is at Home: Ways to Tap Yourself on the Back.**

"10 Ways to Reward Yourself that Won't Bust Your Budget." www.everydollar.com/blog/cheap-ways-to-reward-yourself.

21 **Stay Connected: Online Meeting Etiquette.**

Duffy, Jill. "Top Zoom Tips for Better Videoconferencing in a Locked-Down World" www.pcmag.com/how-to/top-zoom-tips-for-better-videoconferencing-in-a-locked-down-world.

Liu, Joseph. "12 Tips for Making Your Online Meetings More Professional." www.forbes.com/sites/josephliu/2020/03/17/virtual-meeting-tips/#52839e607208.

22 **Stay Connected.**

"How to Stay Connected While Working from Home." www.halfhalftravel.com/remote-work/stay-connected-while-working-from-home.html.

23 **Stay Connected.**

"How to Stay Connected While Working from Home." www.halfhalftravel.com/remote-work/stay-connected-while-working-from-home.html.

24 **Stay Connected.**

"Long Distance Relationships Made Easier." www.lovingfromadistance.com.

25 **Practice Self-Care.**

Hart, Ryan. "40 Fun Things to Do with Empty Notebooks" www.ryanhart.org/notebook-ideas.

26 **Know When to Ask for Help.**

Dizik, Alina. "10 Things to Outsource to A Virtual Assistant." www.entrepreneur.com/slideshow/299695.

Mango Publishing, established in 2014, publishes an eclectic list of books by diverse authors—both new and established voices—on topics ranging from business, personal growth, women's empowerment, LGBTQ studies, health, and spirituality to history, popular culture, time management, decluttering, lifestyle, mental wellness, aging, and sustainable living. We were recently named 2019 **and** 2020's #1 fastest growing independent publisher by *Publishers Weekly*. Our success is driven by our main goal, which is to publish high quality books that will entertain readers as well as make a positive difference in their lives.

Our readers are our most important resource; we value your input, suggestions, and ideas. We'd love to hear from you—after all, we are publishing books for you!

Please stay in touch with us and follow us at:

Facebook: Mango Publishing
Twitter: @MangoPublishing
Instagram: @MangoPublishing
LinkedIn: Mango Publishing
Pinterest: Mango Publishing
Newsletter: mangopublishinggroup.com/newsletter

Join us on Mango's journey to reinvent publishing, one book at a time.